Practical Wisdom
for Software
Professionals

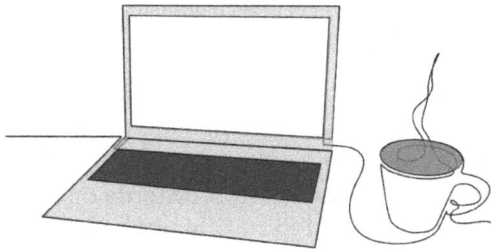

LESSONS LEARNED
as a Software Engineer
in the Real World

James N. Gershfield

Orbitalis
Press

Practical Wisdom for Software Professionals
Lessons Learned as a Software Engineer in the Real World

James N. Gershfield

ISBN-13: 979-8989821709, Paperback

Published by Orbitalis Press, Teaneck NJ, USA
Library of Congress Control Number: 2024946381

First Edition, published in 2024
Orbitalis Press is an imprint of
Scribal Scion Publishing LLC, Teaneck NJ, USA

Visit us at https://orbitalispress.com

Cover photos licensed from Adobe Stock

CONTENTS

Academic Degrees • Acronyms • Age Discrimination

AI • Algorithms • Ants • APIs • Beginning a Job

Behavioral Interviews • Being Too Good • Blockers • Books

Business Analysts • Calculation Versus Computation

Can You Do This? • Career Decisions • Career Progression

Certifications • Cloud Computing

Code, Rinse, Repeat • Comments in Code

Communicating • Commuting

Configuration as Code • Copy Protection • CRMs

Cubicles • Deploying to Production

Desk Location • Difficult to Code or to Use

Disaster and Recovery • Efficiency

Encrypted Laptops • Ending a Job • Estimating

Fads • Financial Incentives • First Impressions

Foul Language and Fist Banging • Fun, Games, and Food

Getting Along • Getting Good at What You Do

Getting the Necessary Experience • Graph Theory

Hidden Code • Holiday Parties

Industry Analysis • Inspiration

Internet of Things–IoT • Interviews • Japan

Job Hopping • Job Location • Job Titles

Knowing Too Much • Lazy Software

Learning a New Codebase • Limiting Questions

Local Experts and How to Deal With Them
Long Lasting Programming Languages
Longevity • Lunch and Learn • Managers
Mathematics and Software • Meaning
Meeting People At Work • Microservices
Mobile Application Development • Obstacles
Office Politics • Open Office Seating • Open Source
Other People's Expectations • Parallel Processing
Part-Time Work • Programming Language Idioms
Quantum Computing • Real Life Software Development
Resume Writing • Retirement - Don't Think About It!
Root Cause Analysis • Saving Ideas for Slow Periods
Self-Confidence • Skills That Should Be Taught in School
Small Versus Large Software • Software Recipes
Sprinting to the Finish • Starting Over
Startups • Statistics and its Importance
Stress Relief • Technical Terms Keep Changing
That's Why They Call It Work
Theory Versus Practice • Things My Managers Taught Me
Trends • Two-Out-of-Three Method • Updating Software
Vacation Time • Version Control
Visual Programming • When Nothing Seems to Work
Why Does the Opening Exist? • Working From Home

Why Read This Book?

Are you contemplating a career as a software engineer or already working in the field, and looking for some practical tips and advice? I worked as a software engineer for over forty years from 1980 to 2022 at companies of all sizes in several industries, and using a variety of software technologies. I am writing this book in 2024 to share some of my experiences and lessons learned, so that you can benefit from them and avoid making the same mistakes that I made.

Other books exist about software careers written by leaders of large companies who managed large teams developing sophisticated software and hardware systems. Those books will give you management's perspective, with a bias toward the business aspects of software technology. Still other books provide an overall career plan for succeeding as a software engineer. And finally there are books that focus on explaining specific technical issues that software engineers face.

This book is different from all of those books because it

- is written from the point of view of a hands-on software engineer working at the senior software engineer level rather than the point of view of corporate management;

- describes real experiences, and lessons learned from those experiences, gained at companies of various sizes and in various industries; and

- describes how software technology has evolved over the last four decades in order to help you develop your own insights into how it might change in the future.

1

Introduction

How many people have experienced hands-on development of computer software continuously from the mid-1970's to now in the year 2024? In the 1970's and 1980's many people got into the field later in life, after working as physicists or mathematicians. Other people got burned out by the stress of constantly changing technology, and switched from computer software to something else midway through their careers. I started working in the software field in 1980 immediately after graduating college with a degree in Computing Science, and I developed software professionally for over forty years without changing careers.

One of the headhunters that I worked with toward the end of my career when I was already in my late 50's told me that I was unlike most people my age in the computer software field. Most people my age that he knew had stopped trying to keep up with changes in technology. They couldn't bring themselves to keep learning and growing. They found it too difficult and stressful.

On the one hand, I wish a book like this had existed when I began my career as a computer programmer. It would have saved me a lot of headaches and aggravation, and it would have helped me to make better decisions throughout my career. On the other hand, software technology has changed so much over the years that it probably would have been impossible for anyone to write this book forty years ago—or even thirty years ago—because the insights that I gained in the course of my career occurred as the technology continuously changed and evolved. In any case, I hope that you can learn from my experiences, both good and bad.

Get your cup of fresh coffee or tea ready, and let's get started!

Experiences and Lessons Learned A-Z

This chapter contains a collection of my experiences and lessons learned. In addition, I have included suggested exercises in some of the sections to help you practice applying those lessons learned to your own situation.

There are also some sections within this chapter containing my thoughts about various aspects of working as a software engineer and how those aspects have changed over the years, without providing specific lessons learned. I think that it is instructive to consider how software development has changed over time. If you are—or want to be—a software engineer you need to be aware of how the field is changing so that you can detect trends as they come and go, and plan for the future.

Due to the rapid rate of change of computer software technology, as you read this book some of the ideas may no longer be completely applicable to your situation, or might have become totally obsolete. But this is the nature of the beast. The most important thing to remember—as in many areas of life—is to keep trying and not to get disappointed and give up. The people who tend to succeed as software engineers are not necessarily the smartest or the most talented, but those who dedicate themselves to continuously striving to be the best software developers they can be throughout their careers.

The sections in this chapter are organized alphabetically to allow you to jump easily from one topic to another. Feel free to read the chapter from start to finish or to move around from section to section as you see fit.

Academic Degrees

What kind of university degree should you get, and how many degrees are enough? I've heard many different viewpoints on this topic, such as "Don't get a PhD degree unless you want to teach in a university or do advanced research", or "It's not the degree, but rather the skills that you have, that matters."

When I was about to graduate from Columbia College with a degree in Computing Science, and one of my professors heard about my plans to work in industry rather than pursue an advanced degree, he was rather upset about the whole idea. He told me that it would be better if I went to graduate school to pursue a PhD in Computer Science and become a professor or researcher. Looking back on it now, perhaps he was right. However, I think that at that time my mind was not mature enough and not disciplined enough to survive the very rigorous mental demands that a PhD would have placed on me. It all depends on the individual.

I think that when I was starting out as a computer programmer in the 1980's, it didn't matter very much whether or not you had a college degree. And it certainly wasn't necessary for your major in college, assuming that you went to college, to be Computer Science. I met many people who were working as computer programmers who had either no college degree, or had majored in a different subject in college such as physics.

In the *old days*, all that mattered was whether you could understand what needed to be implemented in the code, and how to write and test your code so that it would run correctly with as few errors as possible. The skills that were needed to write code were not that difficult to acquire, and if you were an intelligent person with a strong desire to learn, and work hard at improving your coding skills, then you had a place at the table on any computer programming team.

Lessons Learned

If you are considering pursuing a PhD degree in Computer Science and ultimately a career as a professor or researcher, I suggest that you consider how mature your mind is and how disciplined a thinker you are. If you are mainly interested in building functioning software systems, and seeing your lines of code come to life, then probably a master's degree is as far as you should go in your formal university education. But it also depends on the job market and which degrees are in demand.

Exercise

The marketplace for software engineers changes rapidly. Before deciding whether or not to pursue a degree in computer science at the bachelor's, master's, or PhD level, read as many software engineer job descriptions as possible, and see how many of them say that a particular academic degree is required. For example, if the vast majority of ads for a certain job title say that at least a master's degree is required and a PhD is preferred, and you only have a bachelor's degree, perhaps it's time to start looking for a master's degree program.

Acronyms

Many companies make heavy use of acronyms. Some even compile special lists of acronyms and their meanings for employees to use in all of their internal communications. It's just the nature of the beast, and is an unavoidable part of corporate culture.

Most industries have their own set of acronyms, and each company within each industry has its own unique set of acronyms which have developed over time. You need to be careful when you change companies, or industries, because there are many acronyms that mean different things depending on the company and/or the industry. You have to make sure that you are using, and interpreting, acronyms correctly within whichever environment you find yourself.

Lessons Learned

Even though acronyms can be annoying, and difficult to understand, you need to realize that they are just part of real life, and you should allocate some time on a regular basis to learn the acronyms specific to your industry and the unique acronyms within your company. When you join a company, make sure you locate the acronym list and study it carefully.

Exercise

If you haven't already located your company's acronym list, make an effort to find it and keep it handy.

Age Discrimination

Age discrimination is something that I heard a lot about when I was younger, meaning when I was in my 20's and 30's. And I didn't think about it very much until I was near the end of my career. However, I think that age discrimination was there, I just didn't notice it right away. And it changed as I got older. There will be a number of "turning points" in your career where you will need to be on the alert for age discrimination.

One of those turning points occurs when you are working as a software engineer, and you suddenly realize that your managers are younger than you are. It's a weird feeling at first, knowing that the person who is in charge of whether you remain employed at your company, and who has the power to assign you to whatever project they want, in addition to determining your raise and annual bonus, is not as experienced as you are.

Another turning point in one's career happens when you realize that most of your coworkers are a lot younger than you are. What starts to happen is that they tend to socialize with each other, and not with you. They have their own ways of doing things that are different than what you are used to. Many times, they don't want to listen to what older people have to say. There are definitely exceptions to this rule, and I've met a number of people who don't behave that differently to others based on their comparative ages. But once you are at least fifteen or twenty years older than your coworkers, you can expect to start seeing some changes as far as how you are treated by them.

I don't think that there is much you can do about age discrimination when you encounter it. My approach was usually just to ignore it. It's one of those no-win situations in life. If you are one of the older programmers and try to fit in with the younger crowd, you probably won't be accepted no matter what you do. And if you don't try to fit in, you'll probably be seen as unsociable and not a team player.

Lessons Learned

Age discrimination is a fact of life that happens as everyone gets older. Software development teams would benefit greatly if management recognized this fact and took actions to help software engineers of all generations to communicate with each other when working on software projects.

Exercise

If you are a member of a team that consists of older and younger age software developers, try talking with someone who is either significantly older or younger than yourself about your work on the project. You could ask them for feedback about some design decision you made recently, or how they would approach solving some problem that you are facing.

AI

A recent technological trend which has been affecting many areas of society is the increasing use of Artificial Intelligence (AI) in software systems. Let's be honest, however. The term Artificial Intelligence has been around for decades, and people have been developing computer technologies to do many of the things that people do, only faster and better, for many years.

Much of the technology that underlies AI involves what used to be called *neural networks* and is now called *deep learning*. One of the major developments that has occurred recently, and has greatly enhanced the usefulness of deep learning technology is the use of specialized hardware to perform the huge number of calculations that are needed by deep learning systems. One example of that specialized hardware is GPU (Graphics Processing Unit) technology which was developed originally for speeding up computer graphics software. Neural networks have been around for decades, but they weren't able to achieve the kinds of results that we can today because of the previous limitations in computer hardware.

There have been predictions made recently that many of the jobs currently performed by software engineers will be eliminated and replaced by specialized AI software. In my opinion, it remains to be seen how the careers of software engineers will be affected by AI software that's able to generate software code and applications. Over the years of my career I have seen many attempts to streamline the software development process by creating software tools that can generate code. In all of those cases, human intervention was needed in order to make sure that the software tools did the right thing.

9

Algorithms

Algorithms are an important part of programming tests, and job interviews these days inevitably include some kind of technical test that is based on the correct application of algorithms. There are many books and online courses available that help you prepare for taking technical programming tests. But is it really worth spending the time and effort to learn algorithms beyond what you might need to pass those "programming puzzle" tests? My opinion is "Yes, up to a point."

There was a time, long ago, in the 1970's and 1980's, when computer scientists were trying to develop new algorithms for certain mundane tasks like searching for a substring within a string. And they were trying to come up with the fastest one possible. I remember when I was a Computing Science major at Columbia College hearing about someone who was working on a PhD thesis based on a new way of searching for substrings. I don't know whether that kind of algorithm would qualify today as a PhD thesis topic, because by now we have gotten very good at searching for substrings.

As it turns out, searching for things that are parts of other things is extremely important and many applications of this concept have been developed in many industries. Sometimes it's useful to search for certain patterns that repeat and could indicate something significant, especially in scientific or medical data.

In my opinion, learning about algorithms is useful because it forces your brain to think in certain ways that are beneficial for software development. But there are many algorithms that have been developed and optimized for certain common tasks, such as finding all second-level "friends" within your network. Those are the people who are the friends of your friends. If you needed to write some code to do that, you could easily look it up online and find a solution that works.

In fact, one of the major concepts that you need to learn as a professional software engineer is to not reinvent what others have already invented. It just isn't practical to spend long valuable hours developing algorithms for many computing tasks if acceptable solutions already exist.

Lessons Learned

Algorithms are important to learn if you want to excel as a software engineer, and to excel on programming tests. But it will save you a lot of time in your day to day work if you use algorithms that are available online rather then creating them from scratch.

Exercise

Once a month, pick a programming puzzle that you haven't solved before and try solving it. Compare your answer to the answers that are available online. Is yours better or worse?

Ants

Did you know that there are data scientists studying ants in order to learn how to improve AI and data science software?

One of the very interesting developments in data processing in the beginning of the 21st century has been the widespread use of data science to gain insights into masses of data. And many data science PhD students have studied the activities of ants to try to gain insight into how to explore data. Ants seem to have certain ways of moving and exploring an area in order to locate food, and those methods of searching for crumbs of food can be applied somehow to finding meaning in a sea of data.

Amazingly, the biblical book of Proverbs mentions the idea that it's good to avoid being lazy, and it uses ants as an example of creatures that are the opposite of lazy. If you want to be productive, study how ants behave, Proverbs tells us. Not only are ants very active and always moving, but they are also able to work in a coordinated way seemingly with no supervision.

This idea, of a group of workers being coordinated without the need for supervision, is reflected in the modern approach to software development projects. In the old days, a project typically had a project manager and a team lead. The project manager would keep track of things like schedules and budgets. And those folks are still needed to help keep a project on track. However, the need for a team lead has decreased. The ideal project would have no team lead – instead, everyone on the team would work like ants and coordinate their activities with each other.

APIs

Sometimes the simplest things can be difficult to think about when you need to, precisely because they are so basic and fundamental. For example, if you are on a job interview and someone asks you how you would write software to make it easy for customers to access the data and functionality that is hidden within the software, the answer that the interviewer is probably looking for is "Develop an API". Or, perhaps, "Develop multiple API's depending on who will be using it and for what purpose".

So what is an API? The term stands for Application Programming Interface, and when the concept was originally created, it literally meant creating a way for one program to invoke some functionality within another program. Many approaches have been created over the years for inter-program, or inter-system, communication. But in the modern software environment, API's are a broader concept than just providing a way for one program to run some logic in another program.

When you develop large software systems based on the microservices concept, you need to define API's that each microservice can use to access the functionality that is encapsulated within each of the other microservices. API's are an essential part of microservices development. However, there is another very important reason to develop API's, and that is to allow your business customers, and the general public, to access the data and logic that are hidden within your software system. API's are a good example of a software technology that started as a feature with a very narrow focus and expanded over time so that it could be used for multiple purposes. API's are your friend, as they say, so make sure you learn how to use them well!

Beginning a Job

Whether you are just starting a new job or you've been on a job for a while, eventually you will find yourself in the position of being the new person on a team. Aside from the challenges of learning the technical aspects of whatever the project is about, you will find that there could be a number of preexisting relationships between the other members of the team which can make it difficult for you to be seen as an equally valuable coworker. For example, let's say there is a pair of programmers who have worked on a number of projects together, and they have established a certain way of communicating with each other, and a certain way of making technical decisions. If your communication style and decision making process are not aligned with theirs, then there could be a substantial amount of conflict associated with trying to work together.

If you are expecting to begin a new job or join a new team on a project within your current company in the near future, you need to be aware that a major challenge you will face involves becoming a trusted member of the team as quickly as possible. Things to keep in mind are: listening attentively to whatever anyone says, not asking too many questions, learning as much as possible about the project from any documentation that exists, and not taking things personally if someone rejects your suggestions. Above all, try to stay calm and don't get angry.

You have to be very careful when you join a new project, and especially when you are being hired into a company as the lead of a new project, to make sure that the expectations that the company management have and the estimates that they have already made for the project are realistic. If you don't push back

14

on the timeline up front, then it is very likely that the project won't get done on time in the eyes of the manager who is hiring you, and there is a very good chance that you will end up out of a job and working on polishing your shoes and your interviewing skills. If the manager refuses to budge on their estimates even after you point out how unrealistic they are, then you should probably walk away from such an opportunity, and let someone else take it on and put their career at risk.

Lessons Learned

Joining a new team, especially if the team is already part of the way into a project, is one of the most difficult situations that a software engineer can face in their career. Be ready to push back on deadlines that seem to be very unrealistic. If you don't, you could end up being the person blamed for the project not being done on time.

Behavioral Interviews

Interviewing for computer programming jobs has changed drastically during the last four decades. Recently, "behavioral interviews" have become very popular. You need to be prepared to answer the types of questions that are typically asked during behavioral interviews in order to move to the next stage in the interview process. These interviews focus on how you reacted in certain situations, rather than trying to understand how much you know or what you can do.

Once I realized what behavioral interviews are and that I needed to prepare for them, interviewing got much harder for me. You can spend as much time as you want reviewing technical information, and practicing how to write solutions to software puzzles. None of that is going to help you get through a behavioral interview.

Lessons Learned

Behavioral interviews seem to be a fixture of modern job interviews, and you might as well learn how to answer the questions that are asked in those types of interviews.

Exercise

Whenever you experience some kind of challenge that you overcome in your job, make a note of it and add it to the list of experiences that you can talk about during behavioral interviews. It will make it much easier to prepare for those interviews when the time comes.

Being Too Good

There is a trap that you need to watch out for as a software engineer, or anyone for that matter who works in teams. If you get extremely good at whatever it is that you do, your manager might not ever want to let you transfer to another team within the company that you are working for. It's definitely good to become skilled at what you do, but it's also possible to become too good at it, which will make it difficult for you to move around between projects. If you find yourself in this trap, you might need to look for another job in order to switch to a different project that will give you an opportunity to learn something new.

I have seen people end up in this kind of situation in their careers, especially at large companies where people become acclimated to doing things a certain way, "because that's how we always did it." In smaller companies, or companies that haven't been in existence for very long, things tend to be more fluid and it's typically easier to move around from one team to another.

Lessons Learned

Although it might seem counterintuitive, it's not good to become too much of an expert at what you do unless you love it so much that you just don't want to ever do anything else. Perhaps it can be compared to an actor who performs so amazingly well in one particular movie role that they will never be considered for any other movie roles in the future.

Exercise

Every few months, ask yourself whether you would be able to step into a different role if your job ended suddenly.

Blockers

A fairly recent phenomenon is the daily so-called *standup meeting*, which involves each member of the team saying the following three things: (1) what I accomplished yesterday, (2) what I plan to accomplish today, and (3) whether there are any *blockers* that are preventing me from doing what I need to do.

The first two items are pretty straightforward, but the third item can be tricky. Is there something truly blocking you from doing your work, or have you merely not figured out how to go around any obstacles that seem to be in your way? Take the initiative to figure out how to get your work done without being impeded by external forces. Advanced planning also can help you to avoid being blocked by others or by the circumstances. Being blocked can occur at many levels and can occur frequently. Longer term work such as self-development can also be blocked.

Lessons Learned

You have multiple responsibilities when it comes to being blocked. You need to always be on the lookout for current blockers that are interfering with your productivity on your project, blockers that may materialize in the future, and things that are blocking you from achieving your long-term goals, and figure out how to either eliminate them or go around them.

Exercise

Every morning before starting your workday, think for a few minutes about what things are preventing you from getting your work done that day. Once a week, think about your long-term goals and what might be blocking you from achieving them.

Books

In addition to the nature of software changing over the years, the need for books about software development has also changed. There is so much technical information available now online that you might think that there is no need for computer software books anymore. Apparently that doesn't seem to be the case, since there are still a number of companies that keep publishing new books on software topics year after year, and people keep buying their books.

It can be very tempting to buy a book about a technical software topic when the need arises. When I was working at AT&T Bell Labs in the 1980's, I was interested in learning something about the Apple Macintosh computer, which had been around for only a few years at that point. I had already become accustomed to buying computer books whenever I needed to learn anything about a particular computer technology, so the thought immediately popped into my head to search for a book on the Macintosh computer in my local bookstore.

You have to remember that back in the 1980's and early 1990's there wasn't any easy way to buy books online, and you couldn't easily search the Internet for technical information about computer technology in the way that you can today. If you wanted to find a book on your topic, you had to go to a brick and mortar bookstore and search through the aisles of books for a book on your topic.

At one bookstore that I frequented, I found a small book titled something like "How to Use the Macintosh". After I bought it and showed it to one of my colleagues at Bell Labs, the comment

I received was similar to "Why on earth would you buy a book on how to use the Macintosh? The whole point of the Macintosh is that it is so easy to use that you don't need to buy a book about how to use it." Well, it would have been nice if I had known that before I bought the book, but not knowing how easy it was to use that computer I assumed that I needed to read a book to learn how to use it.

Luckily, nowadays if you want to learn about almost any topic in computer science all you have to do is go online and search for some basic information. Then you can decide whether or not it's worth the money to buy a book on the topic.

Sometimes you might need to read a book about a certain topic for your job, and you notice that one of your colleagues just happens to own a book that would be perfect to read. I have found that a best practice when it comes to borrowing and lending books at work is to avoid doing it. Books tend to disappear, and once you lend a book to someone else, there is a good chance that you won't ever see the book again. If you think that you could benefit from a certain book, buy your own copy.

My experience, in general, with using public libraries to find helpful books on computer technology has not been very good. The main problem as I see it with the books in public libraries is that it is difficult for libraries to keep up with the rapid changes in computer technology. Libraries have limited budgets for purchasing new books, and the rate at which new books are released on computer topics is so rapid that almost as soon as a book is purchased, there is another book about to be released on the latest version of the software or hardware. Books on computer subjects become either partially or completely obsolete very quickly.

If you find yourself needing to read a lot of books on many different computer software topics, it might be worth looking into subscribing to one of the online software book publishers, where for one annual fee you get unlimited online access to all of the books that they publish.

Lessons Learned

Before buying a book on a technical topic in computer science, first do an online search and see whether you can find some basic information about that topic. If you can find the information you need online, then just use that information and save yourself the cost of a book. If the information is not sufficiently detailed or is not easy to understand, then by all means look for books on the subject that you can consider purchasing.

Business Analysts

Business Analysts are the people on a project who figure out what the requirements of a software application are. And it is their responsibility to write the requirements documents that specify what the application should do, mainly from a business perspective but to a certain extent from a technical perspective as well. The requirements typically include user interface specifications, web site page layouts, and other things.

One problem that I have seen occurs when there are two or more business analysts on the same project with the same level of authority to write the requirements documents. One large project that I was on had two analysts writing requirements. I think this occurred because a tight deadline had been imposed by the application development manager. The thought was that two analysts could divide the work and write the documents faster.

What actually happened was that the two analysts couldn't agree on various aspects of the requirements development process. They had different opinions about things like document formatting and level of detail. The end result was that instead of accelerating the requirements writing process, the opposite occurred. And confusion ensued regarding the application's intended functionality, and this made it harder for the software engineers to get the application done on time.

Lessons Learned

If you find yourself on a project that has more than one person responsible for defining the application requirements, beware. Your project could be headed for failure, or at least a lot of confusion and delays.

Calculation Versus Computation

There are some interesting problems in computer science where you need to determine a certain value, but there are two fundamentally different ways to accomplish the same goal. One way is to use mathematics to derive a formula that determines the answer by plugging in the appropriate values into the variables in the formula. This approach is generally called *calculation*. The other way is to develop an algorithm that is a series of steps that will determine the answer after running the algorithm as a computer program. This approach is called *computation*.

Only a limited set of problems can be solved by creating a mathematical formula to calculate the answer, but if you can then usually you will be able to determine the resulting value much faster than executing a program that implements an algorithm that computes the answer via a repeated set of operations.

One such problem is to determine how many prime numbers exist within a certain range of numbers. If you had a formula, you could just plug in the two numbers that represent the lower end and upper end of the range, and run a program that calculates the formula. Without a formula to calculate, you would need to determine all of the prime numbers that exist within the given range of numbers, and then count how many prime numbers you found. This could take a very long time if the range of numbers is very large.

Can You Do This?

What should you do if an opportunity presents itself but you feel that you are not qualified to do the work? What I have done in this situation is to quickly learn enough so that I can start doing the work, understanding that I will learn the rest on the job.

This approach is the same one that is used by many salespeople who see an opportunity to sell a new product. If they take too long to learn all aspects of the product and become a leading expert, the opportunity will disappear. Ultimately, it's a balancing act between how much you know already and how much you still need to learn in order to do the job.

Certifications are helpful in this situation because they force you to learn a certain amount about a subject and pass a test. You aren't necessarily an expert just because you got the certification but you gain highly relevant knowledge. Combined with your other experience, they help make you more competitive.

Lessons Learned

If a great opportunity presents itself but you aren't an expert, rapidly learn enough to start the project, and keep learning on the job. This approach works best for employees rather than contractors or consultants, unless the project is very long term.

Exercise

Pick a new skill that you don't have experience with and try to get up to speed on it within a few days. Then, try writing some code that uses that skill. Ask someone who already has the experience to rate your work.

Career Decisions

There are a number of important decisions that every software engineer needs to make throughout their career. Here are some of them with their pros and cons.

Company Size: Small, Medium or Large

One of the benefits of working at small companies is that you have the opportunity to get to know the top management within the company, including sometimes even the president and CEO. In some ways, this is a good thing, because it lets you have more input into the discussions that the top management is having. On the other hand, it can also be a bad thing, especially if the leader of the company has various negative personal qualities.

Company Type: Consulting or Non-Consulting

My experience has been that there is a major difference in mindset within consulting companies compared to non-consulting companies. Consulting companies tend to be much more project focused, for example developing an application for a client to solve a specific problem. Non-consulting companies also have projects, but their projects tend to serve the needs of the internal departments of the company, and are more company focused as a result.

Generalist or Specialist

In the field of computer software, there are generalists and there are specialists. They both have their place in the industry, but they have their own characteristics and their own unique challenges and rewards. The question that you need to answer is, "Should I specialize in something or just be a generalist?"

And if you decide that you want to be a specialist, you then need to answer the question, "Which specialty should I focus on?" I suppose this is the same kind of question that people face in many other careers also, such as medicine, law, engineering and architecture.

After many years in the software industry, my own feeling is that it is good to specialize in something, but to maintain at least a good level of skill in software engineering in general. Doing so will help you pivot to a different specialty in the future if conditions change and you decide that you want to change your area of specialty. If you have a decent background in many areas of software, then switching your focus will be that much easier. In addition, you may be forced to change your area of focus as technologies develop, mature and become obsolete, and as new market forces come into play.

Front End or Back End

When I started out in computer programming, there wasn't very much work available in designing front ends for applications, since the operating system at that time didn't support graphical user interfaces very well. The IBM mainframe computers used text-based user interfaces, as did the minicomputers that were sold in the 1980's.

In fact, one of my last projects that I worked on as an employee at AT&T was a document editing product that integrated a scanner with the ability to place text and simple graphics like rectangles and circles within the same document. We were developing the product on MS-DOS, and had to do a lot of graphics programming to achieve the results. While I was on that project, I remember hearing about some new technology called Windows that was being developed at Microsoft Corporation in the 1980's, and that would revolutionize the use of personal computers. Needless to say, it wasn't long before we needed to rewrite our code to run within the Windows operating system.

Over the years, the specialties of front end coding and back end coding have merged into the specialty of web development. It's not enough any more to be only a front end coder, or only a back end coder. Companies want software engineers who can do both things well. I discovered that at one of my jobs where I was focused mainly on back end coding while working on web application development, and was told that if I wanted to continue advancing in my career at that company I would need to develop my front end coding skills as well.

Industry

One thing that didn't occur to me when I was starting out in my career was the significance of the industry that you will be working in. When you are in school studying computer science, you tend to focus on the material that you are studying, whether it's algorithms, programming languages or other technical aspects. It probably won't occur to you that once you get a job, that job will be within a specific company, and more importantly, within a specific industry. While the specific company you end up working for can determine many aspects of your experiences on the job, the industry that the company is in can potentially be even more significant.

It is extremely important to understand something about the industry that you will be working in, not just the company. There is certain business knowledge that is important to know about each industry, and knowing that information can make a big difference in how successful you will be at your job.

Structured or Unstructured Environment

Some people prefer to work in an environment where the work is relatively structured, while others prefer to work in a relatively unstructured environment. It's important for you to know which group of people you fall into. It can be very frustrating for someone who likes to know what they will be working on, when, how and with whom, to be put on a project where there is very little structure, and things can change in an instant. Similarly, some who enjoys and thrives on projects where things are very fluid and can change quickly will find it very stifling to work on a highly structured project. If you aren't sure which type of person you are, you might need to experience both types of environments and then see which one you feel most comfortable working in.

Lessons Learned

If you are interested in working in the area of web application development, don't limit yourself to only front end coding or back end coding. You need to develop your skills in both areas. Many people find one or the other of those skills more enjoyable, so you need to be ready to force yourself to get better at whichever skill you are not so interested in. Just tell yourself that if you want to stay employed as a software engineer in the web development area, you need to keep getting better at both skills.

Career Progression

As you move through your career as a software engineer, you will be faced with various choices and decisions that you will need to make. Some of these just can't be avoided, and trying to avoid making a decision will itself end up being a decision.

One of the things that any software engineer or manager needs to consider is whether to stay at the same company for a long time, or to move around from one company to another during the course of their career.

Of course, I am assuming that the person has a choice in the matter. Sometimes, these kinds of things are beyond one's control, and even if you wanted to stay at the same company for a long time, sometimes that is just impossible. For example, consider the situation where a company splits into several smaller companies, such as what happened to AT&T and the Bell System back in the mid-1980's. Or sometimes a company experiences a downturn in revenue or earnings and decides to lay off a portion of its workforce.

Assuming that you have a choice to stay at your current company, I think the question is an important one: Is it better to stay at the same company for a long time, or is it better to change companies every now and then? There are pros and cons to both options. Staying at the same company can give you an opportunity to grow within a familiar environment, while changing companies frequently can give you a variety of experiences that could be useful in the future. Conversely, staying at the same company too long can limit your growth, since many companies tend to keep using the same technologies for long periods of time after making large investments in them. And changing companies too frequently can make it hard to develop strong personal relationships with your peers.

Getting involved with online developer groups can help make it easier to develop long-term relationships with other software developers regardless of where you happen to be working. I've known software engineers who regularly contributed answers to questions on the online technical discussion websites. Doing so helped them to become well known within the software engineer community. In fact, if you want to break into a new area of software technology a good way to do that is to become active on one of the many online technical communities.

Lessons Learned

Navigating your career as the years go by is a never-ending balancing act. If you stay too long at a company it could hurt your career. But not staying long enough could also do damage. One thing I think is clear: The more you are involved with the software development community outside of your current job, the better you will be able to navigate the future as it unfolds.

Exercise

If you are not currently an active participant in at least one or two online software developer communities, pick one and get started reading other people's posts and submitting your own posts. Doing so will open up a whole world of new friends and new opportunities.

Certifications

Are software certifications worth the time and money? This topic has been fiercely debated for many years, both pro and con. My own opinion is that it depends on what your goals are and what your circumstances are. Let me explain.

If you are hoping to land a job which requires candidates to be adept in a specific technology, and a certification exists for that technology, it makes sense to get the certification if you don't have it already. A long time ago, it probably didn't matter that much whether you had a certification, and the main thing that mattered was your experience. But these days having a certification could help you get past the resume filtering software that prevents job seekers from getting their resumes in front of hiring managers. And having a certification in the specific technology or skill that the hiring company is looking for helps support your credibility when you claim that you are qualified in that area.

Sometimes companies expect their employees to achieve certain certifications because of relationships that they have with particular software vendors, and those companies need to show that they have at least a certain percentage of employees who are certified in that vendor's software products. If you are already working in one of those companies, you can help make your job more secure by getting those certifications.

Preparing for software certifications can be very stressful. Unless you really know the subject matter extremely well, you never know for sure whether or not you will be successful in passing the test and getting the certification. Even though the percentage of correct answers for many of the software certifications that exist is not very high, typically in the sixty-five to seventy-five percent range, some of the certification tests are very difficult. That could explain why the percentage of correct answers required to pass the test is in that range and not higher. I remember when I was in college, unless the professor was "grading on a curve", in order to get a top grade for the course you needed to get above ninety percent correct on midterm and final exams. But when it comes to industry certifications, it seems that almost none of them requires above an eighty percent correct answer rate.

I don't think that people generally ask certified software engineers exactly what score they got on any particular certification exam, so if you are getting certified in order to help you get a job interview, or get a job offer, all that really matters usually is whether or not you are able to pass the test and get the certification.

Depending on which certification you are trying to achieve, there could be a lot of information online about the content of the test and what kinds of questions you will be asked, and so on. Some of the companies offering software certifications have practice test available, many times for a small fee, which you can use to test yourself and see where your weaknesses are. There are also many courses online for many of the more common certifications. I found it very useful to take practice tests when preparing for a certification exam because it helped me determine which areas I was weak in and needed to focus my studying on.

Before registering to take a certification test, you should check whether you will be allowed to take the test again, and within what time period. Also, you should find out whether or not you will be required to pay an additional fee to retake the test. Some companies allow you to take their certification test up to two or three times for one fee. You should always check the latest information before registering for any certification test. Also, sometimes a certification will get updated and there will be a new version of the certification test available. Always check whether this is the case, before registering for any certification exam.

Lessons Learned

If you are a software engineer who works with any of the major modern technologies such as cloud computing, data engineering, or data science, you should plan on allocating some time and money each year to study for and to take the latest versions of the related certification exams. Even if you don't need to acquire any new certifications, they tend to expire after two or three years and you will need to renew the certifications by taking the exams again.

Cloud Computing

The term cloud computing refers to running your software applications on a hardware infrastructure that is not located in your own facilities. Instead, your software runs on servers that are located in the cloud service provider's facilities. This is a very large oversimplification of what cloud computing is, but it gives you the basic idea. Cloud computing is one of the most significant developments in computer infrastructure to be created within the last couple of decades. The whole field of cloud computing is vast and it can take years for the average person to become highly skilled.

Given the vastness of cloud computing, I'll only mention a few of the innovations that cloud computing has brought to computers and software, and which I feel are very significant in the history of computing.

Virtual Servers

The idea of a virtual servers existed before the recent growth of cloud computing. However, the ability to easily create, start, stop, and destroy them whenever needed is something that cloud computing companies have innovated. The reason this is significant is because even though the cost to run a virtual server is considerably less than the cost of purchasing and running a real server, they are not free. Typically, the customer is charged a fee for each minute of fraction of a minute of time that the virtual server exists and is running. If they were left running all the time, the costs would be rather large. Modern cloud computing environments allow you to automatically create, start, stop, and destroy virtual servers as needed. In fact, it's possible to automate the creation and deletion of an entire operating environment including databases, networking, virtual servers, and application software whenever needed.

As an example, suppose your company needed to run a set of sophisticated reports every evening. But in order to run the reports you needed to import data from a multitude of data sources, run various programs to analyze the data, and then run other programs to generate reports from the data. Instead of setting up multiple permanent virtual servers with application software to run all of the data analysis and reporting software, you could set up an automated process that would run every night, create all of the virtual servers, load all of the applications into the virtual servers, run the applications, and store the resulting reports in a repository for future access. Once all of the applications were finished running, the automated process would shut down all of the servers and delete them. If the entire process took six hours from start to finish, you would only pay for the six hours that all of that infrastructure existed each night. That's a savings of seventy-five percent compared to keeping all of those virtual servers running all day every day.

Containerization

Another technology that existed before the recent boom in cloud computing is containerization. But with the advent of cloud computing, containerization has become an even more valuable technology. Containerization is a way of bundling together software applications and all of the files that they need to function correctly. It also simplifies the deployment of software applications, both the executable code that software engineers write and the library files that the programming language needs to run the application code. And of course containers can be deployed, started, stopped, and destroyed automatically in a cloud environment.

Serverless Computing

Having essentially eliminated the need for companies to own their own hardware infrastructure, cloud computing has gone a step further and created things called serverless functions. The feature that Amazon AWS has that supports this concept is called Lambda functions. A Lambda function is a small piece of code that can be written in any one of several programming languages, and which is executed on demand when triggered by a specified event. The code in a Lambda function is executed on a virtual server somewhere in the cloud, but typically there is no way to control exactly where it is executed. One of the potential drawbacks of this design is that it could present a security risk since the exact server is not known, and a company's data security policy might require that the precise location of all servers be known whenever their software is run.

There are several advantages to creating AWS Lambda functions. First, no explicit configuration of servers is needed, not even virtual servers. Second, there is no cost to set up a Lambda function, and charges are only incurred when the Lambda function is executed. So, they are very easy to write and deploy.

You might be wondering, "Are there any downsides to Lambda functions?" Based on my experience, the answer is "Yes". The main downside that I have found is that even though the cost to execute the function one time is very low, the costs can add up and become quite large if the function is executed too many times. It's like eating a low-calorie snack, thinking that doing so will help one lose weight. That's true only if one eats the snack infrequently. Even a low calorie snack will become a diet buster if it's consumed too much. The same is true for Lambda functions.

One example of using a Lambda function this way in a cloud environment would be if an API were designed for processing IoT (Internet of Things) data transmissions. One can imagine that there might be millions of data points being transmitted every day from various devices to a back-end cloud-based software service. If a Lambda function were invoked for every item of data, then the total cost of executing the Lambda function would be prohibitive. In that case, it would be much more economical to configure one or more virtual servers and run code on them, perhaps using one of the popular back-end code frameworks, to process the individual transmissions of IoT data.

Hybrid and Multi-Vendor Cloud Implementations

Many companies have been coverting their server-based applications to become cloud-based. However, there are some situations where a company's servers need to remain and be able to work together with some cloud-based applications. This is known as a hybrid configuration. Also, many companies are starting to use multiple cloud vendors and need to understand how to implement applications across multiple cloud systems.

Lessons Learned

Cloud computing has evolved over the past ten to fifteen years to become one of the most important technological innovations ever in the field of computer software. If you haven't worked with any of the major cloud computing services, you should start as soon as possible to learn about them and get some experience developing applications that can run in a cloud environment.

Code, Rinse, Repeat

One thing that I've seen companies do that can be very successful and lucrative is to modify an existing software application or tool to satisfy the special needs of a specific customer or client, and then make those features available to all other current and future customers.

One of the companies that I interviewed for had created a specialized application for one customer, and they made sure that the licensing agreement permitted the company to use the features that they developed for that customer in future versions of the application. As time went on, new customers wanted the application, but they needed a few customizations in order for the software to work for their unique business situation. The software company did the customizations and charged the customer for those customizations.

Lessons Learned

One of the great things about creating custom features for a particular customer who is willing to pay you to develop it for them, as long as they agree to allow you to sell those custom features to future customers, is that the cost of enhancing a product that you already have for sale is borne either in part or in full by a paying customer. That customer is happy because they get the additional functionality that they need in your software, and you are happy because you can then increase the size of your potential market for your software. It's one of those so-called "win-win" scenarios.

Comments in Code

Every computer programming language that I know of has a feature that allows the programmer to embed explanatory comments within the source code that they write. It's been like that for many years. Only very low-level computer languages like assembly language don't provide a way to embed comments in code.

Interestingly, there has been a debate among software developers that has been raging for decades whether or not to use that feature and include comments within your code. There are good arguments on both sides of the question. Reasons to use comments include: (1) helping other programmers to read and understand your code, (2) providing for a place to put important information relating to the code such as why the code was written a certain way. Those who are opposed to the idea of embedding comments in code argue that comments can: (1) become outdated if the code changes, and (2) be more difficult to understand than just reading the code.

I don't expect the debate to ever be completely settled, however the trend at the time of writing this book seems to be moving toward the idea that code should be written in such a way that it is self-explanatory. Software engineers shouldn't have to worry whether a comment that was written a year ago still applies to the code today and has not become obsolete.

Lessons Learned

Try to write your code so that it is easy to read and understand. That should make everyone happy on both sides of the debate.

Communicating

One of the most important aspects of a computer software career is communicating with others on your team and within your company. The following are some of my experiences and lessons learned in this area.

Presentations

I remember having to prepare my first presentation to the other members of my group. In those days we used something called an "overhead projector" and we had to create plastic "slides" that would be place on top of a glass panel that had a light source underneath it, and would project the image onto the wall or a screen.

After creating a set of slides, one of my co-workers took one look at them and said that I needed to spiffy them up a bit. They had no color, no graphics at all. What I had done was create a set of slides with a title and a set of bullet points for each slide. My co-worker suggested at least adding a color background to the title area, and a different color background to the bullet point area, which is what I did. The updated slides didn't look amazing, but they did look a lot more visually appealing than my original slides.

I also remember one of our group members giving a presentation about a new workflow that we were going to start following in our jobs. After giving a brief introduction to the presentation, the speaker said: "And now I want to show you a simple diagram of the workflow". The diagram that was shown was extremely complicated and had at least 15 or 20 boxes connected by many arrows. Needless to say, the reaction from the group was not very positive.

When you make technical presentations, always make sure to make them visually appealing. And don't put too much information on each page..

Prioritize This

I noticed recently that a lot of people say "Let's prioritize this". When people used to say that it meant that they wanted to go through the process of prioritizing a set of goals, or deliverables. That is, they wanted to figure out which items were the "high priority" items, and which were the lower priority items. But now, a lot of people use that expression to mean that they want to assign a high priority to a particular thing. It can be very confusing to people who have been in the industry a long time. Something to keep in mind for those more experienced software engineers who remember life before the Internet.

Lessons Learned

Be sensitive to the way that different people use certain words, and try to be flexible in how you use those words. If someone tends to use a word incorrectly but it is clear what they mean, it's not worth trying to teach them correct grammar and usage.

Analogies

One thing I've noticed while working on the job is that there are some people who are not able to think in terms of analogies. And if you try to tell them something in the form of an analogy they just can't understand what you are trying to say, no matter how hard you keep trying to explain to them what you mean.

For example, I was on a project where we had done something a certain way in the past for another project and it worked out rather well. I thought that it would be helpful in our current project to do something similar. When I tried to tell this to my boss, his response was like "No, we can't do that on this project because we aren't doing that on this project." I tried to explain that I was just making an analogy – "just as on that project we were faced with such and such an obstacle, and we did such and such and it helped out a lot, similarly on this project we could do something similar. Not exactly the same thing, just something similar". After trying a couple of times to explain that I didn't mean that we should do exactly the same thing that we did on the other project, I gave up and concluded that my boss was just unable to think in terms of analogies.

It's interesting to note that one of the major college admissions testing companies recently removed the analogy as one of the categories of questions in the verbal part of the tests. Perhaps this was because they realized that a lot of people have a very difficult time thinking in those terms. It is unfortunate that not everyone is able to think comfortably in terms of analogies – it can be a very good way of explaining an idea and thinking about how to solve a problem.

Lessons Learned

Try to avoid using analogies when speaking with people at work, unless you have determined ahead of time that they are capable of thinking that way. Otherwise, you will probably have some unpleasant experiences when discussing project-related issues with your co-workers and boss.

Don't Get Defensive

One of the "traps" that I have gotten into a number of times in my career was responding to accusations of "being defensive" when talking about something. Eventually, I caught on, and now I know how to handle this kind of situation better. But until I learned how to handle it, I really didn't enjoy the experience.

What can happen is that someone will accuse you of being defensive after they say something negative about your performance or your behavior. If you respond by denying what they are saying, or acting as though you are annoyed by what they are saying, then they will immediately say, "See, look, you are getting defensive right now!" I came to the conclusion that the best way to respond accusations of being defensive is to just say "thank you for letting me know", and not say any more. In my mind, it's really just a game that some people play to try to get you to look bad. You need to be prepared to say the right thing so that you don't fall into their verbal trap.

Lessons Learned

If someone accuses you of responding to criticism in a defensive way, just smile and say, "Thanks for letting me know". Don't fall into their verbal "you're being defensive" trap!

Talk With Your Manager Before Taking Action

One thing I learned the hard way was the idea of letting your manager know if you are thinking about switching to another project or department within the same company. What happened to me was that my manager was happy with my work and was considering promoting me to a manager of a technical team. I had been looking into switching to another project within the same company because I was looking to get some other experience. Little did I know that my manager was planning to recommend me for a promotion. Before he had a chance to tell me about it, I had already spoken with the manager of the other project and made arrangements to move to the other project. When I told my current manager about my planned switch, he was disappointed that I hadn't spoken with him first and I hadn't even given him an opportunity to let me know what he had in mind for me.

Lessons Learned

Before you make a commitment to switch to another project or department within your current company, make sure to discuss the idea with your current manager. You never know what he or she might be planning for you, and just hasn't gotten around to telling you yet.

Keeping your client informed

No matter how hard you try to complete your coding and testing by a given deadline, there will be times when you won't be able to. I've found that the best thing to do in these situations is to communicate clearly what went wrong, why the coding wasn't finished on time, and what you will do differently in the future to avoid the same thing happening again.

Lessons Learned

Owning your mistakes and communicating clearly what went wrong will cause people to respect you more than if you tried to conceal problems. Always indicate how you plan to fix the problem and ensure that it won't happen again.

Commuting

As I write this in 2024, the trend among companies that hire software engineers seems to be shifting toward requiring employees to come into the office at least a few days per week. Unfortunately, the cost of commuting has risen tremendously during the last few years, due to high prices for gas, the ever-rising cost of the cars themselves, and the cost of car insurance.

It might seem obvious that companies that require employees to commute into the office would provide sufficient parking for employees. However I have been in situations where there wasn't enough parking for all of the employees, and it caused a lot of headaches and problems.

Another annoyance related to parking that I encountered in my career was that, even though there was enough parking for everyone who worked at the building, the best parking spaces were reserved for the management. In the worst situation like this that I can remember, a very large number of parking spaces surrounding the building were reserved for management, causing non-managers to have to walk long distances to get from their car into the building.

Lessons Learned

Before taking a job where you will need to commute to work by car, make sure that there will be enough parking space available for everyone who works at the location. Otherwise, you could be facing constant stress regarding where you will be able to park without having to worry about your car getting towed.

Configuration as Code

A very interesting way of writing code that has become very popular within recent years is the creation of configuration descriptions. The idea is that instead of writing code to do something, you just write a description of what you want, and behind the scenes there is a software application that regularly checks your description and makes the necessary updates to whatever the description is about.

Tools such as Terraform and Puppet let you create one or more files containing detailed descriptions of your computer network, deployed applications, and so on, and they read those files on a regular basis and automatically update your deployed environment to match the descriptions in the files.

Another common use for configuration descriptions is in the area of APIs and how they are defined. There are tools that have been developed, such as Swagger, that let you define the API configurations and allow other tools to generate code that will implement the API functions.

Lessons Learned

Learning how to use configuration tools can be very helpful in the career of a software engineer. It might not seem that important because it doesn't involved writing logical statements using a regular programming language. But in modern software applications that can involve dozens of servers, networks, databases, containers, and many other kinds of components, knowing how to keep all of those things configure correctly using modern configuration tools is a critical skill that should not be ignored.

Copy Protection

Since the very early days of software for personal computers, people have been trying to make copies of software without paying for it, and companies that produced the software have been trying to prevent people from making copies of the software. This went on for decades, and is still going on, although in a somewhat different way.

For some reason, many people thought that it was perfectly OK to copy software for personal computers without paying for it, even though they knew that it was violating the copyright laws. In the early days of the personal computer, It was relatively easy to copy software, and it was very difficult for the companies that developed and sold the software applications to do anything about it. Eventually, companies started to realize the they needed to at least try to do something to stop all of the illegal copying of software because so many people were using their software without paying for it.

Trying to prevent users from unauthorized copying of software is a great example of a cycle that can go on for decades. People try to evade the current copy protection schemes, so companies respond by implementing new techniques. Then, the people trying to do the unauthorized copying work to evade the copy protection schemes, and it goes on and on.

Lessons Learned

Keep an eye out for various cycles that develop that are similar to the copy protection cycles. You might be able to build a career by working on them.

CRMs

There is a type of software application that virtually all businesses, of at least a certain size, will purchase. That type of software is called a CRM, which is an abbreviation for Customer Record Management system. CRM systems are usually very large, very complex, and usually very expensive pieces of software. Why do companies spend the money on CRM systems? Because they can store all of their valuable information about their customers, products and sales in the same system in an organized way.

But CRM systems also have disadvantages. One of the biggest disadvantages of a CRM system is that after a company spends money licensing, installing, and configuring a new CRM system, it will need to spend a large amount of money to maintain the software moving forward.

One of the costliest of maintenance activities involves major upgrades to the CRM software, because the data might need to be migrated from the old version to the new version. Unfortunately, migrating data from an older version of a CRM to a newer version often times cannot be done automatically as part of the software upgrade. It might require hiring a consulting company who specializes in the specific CRM system that the company licenses.

This is great for those consulting companies who provide the CRM migration services, but it's not so great for the companies that license the CRM software. In addition to the costs, if the data migration is not done one-hundred percent correctly the resulting data could cause problems for the company. Since companies rely so heavily on their CRM systems providing the correct data at the correct time, if even a small amount of the data in their

CRM system is wrong, it could cost the company a lot of money in lost sales or other issues.

Another common activity that software engineers engage in relating to CRM systems is creating customizations for each client that is using the CRM. The business processes of large companies are usually so complex that the out-of-the-box features of a typical CRM system won't satisfy the company's need without a large amount of customization. And all of those customizations cost money.

Lessons Learned

Since CRMs are such complicated pieces of software, it's been possible for software professionals to build entire careers on customizing, maintaining, upgrading, and migrating CRM systems. If you enjoy doing that kind of work, perhaps you should consider learning about CRM systems and getting certified on one or more of the major ones.

Cubicles

Cubicles evolved over time. A lot of people who have gotten into the software field recently probably don't even know what a cubicle is. A long time ago, computer programmers actually had offices, or shared an office with one or more other programmers. Eventually, only managers or senior team leaders were entitled to have an office or to share an office. To save costs, companies started using things called cubicles, which were prefabricated work areas that had walls as tall as people, and an opening to enter and exit. Each cubicle had a reasonably large amount of space, perhaps eight by eight feet.

As time went on, and companies looked for more ways to reduce costs as a way of increasing profitability, the size of cubicles kept shrinking. I remember that cubicles went from around eight by eight feet to seven by seven feet. I eventually ended up in a six by six foot cubicle. And the height of the cubicle walls kept decreasing to the point that the walls were only several inches above the top of the desk inside the cubicle.

Nowadays, many companies have adopted the *open space* concept in office furniture, which means that cubicles have been replaced by rows of long tables with no dividers or separation of any kind between programmers, and of course almost no privacy. Personally, I found open space work environments to be very uncomfortable and made it difficult to focus on my programming work, which usually requires a lot of concentration.

One funny thing happened to me in one of my jobs. I had gotten used to working in a six by six foot work area, which was just big enough to enclose a desk and chair, and the desk surface was just large enough to hold a desktop computer, one or two monitors, a mouse, and a telephone. When I left that job and started my next job, I was assigned my own small office, which was pretty amazing considering the evolution of office cubicles at the time. The office was around eight feet by ten feet or so. But instead of using all of the space in the office, I only used the space equivalent to a six by six foot cubicle. One day it dawned on me that I was limiting my use of the space in my office to the space in a six by six foot cubicle because I had gotten used to that limitation in my previous job. I artificially constrained myself to that amount of space, even though I didn't need to.

After several months, I realized that I could spread out a bit, which I did. That experience taught me that people are very good at making do with less and less, and sometimes don't even realize that they don't need to limit themselves so much when circumstances change.

Lessons Learned

If you, as a software engineer, have a hard time concentrating in a work environment where there are a lot of distractions and nothing to shield your eyes from all of the activity going on in the office, you might want to consider trying to find a company that will allow you to work in a cubicle-like workspace. Companies would probably benefit from offering a choice to their software developers between open space and cubicle workspaces instead of forcing them to work in an open space environment.

Deploying to Production

It might seem like a relatively simple thing to do: After you finish testing the new version of your code in a development environment and in a test environment, you want to deploy the code to your production environment. The problem that I've seen happen over and over is that the development, testing and production environments are not exactly the same. Development and testing environments tend to be very similar, although there might be some differences. But the testing and production environments frequently are very different from each other, and in some very significant ways.

You might ask yourself, why would a company create development, testing and production environments, and then not make sure that they are configured identically? Typically, the answer, which affects many things within companies, involves money. Modern computing environments tend to have multiple servers to be able to handle very large quantities of data. However, setting up an environment with lots of servers, and all of the other features that are needed to support a large collection of servers, is a relatively expensive thing to do.

If you have a limited budget, which is usually the case in a corporate environment, you have to decide where to spend the money. Your production environment has top priority because that's where the software will run that your customers and clients will use to interact with your applications. So, you want to make sure that your production environments have the most powerful and reliable collections of servers possible. That means that you will have less money to spend on the lower priority environments, namely your development and testing environments.

The number of different environments that are used for development, testing, and production can vary greatly from one company to the next. Some companies might only have a development environment in which all coding and testing take place, and a production environment. At the other end of the spectrum are companies that have multiple development environments, multiple test environments for things like integration testing, beta testing, and performance testing, and multiple production environments. In general, having more environments available for software development makes it easier to control the flow of the software from development to production.

Lessons Learned

The number of development environments available to software engineers can have a significant impact on the software development. If you are looking for a new job or a new project, it would be wise to ask how many environments there are and how similar the environments are to each other.

Desk Location

One thing that you need to realize when you start a new job is that you are the *new person*. This means that most likely all of the good desk locations are already taken by other members of the staff. I have been in a few situations where my seating location was really bad, and it affected the quality of my work.

One situation involved being seated in a cubicle that was directly across from the manager in charge of the software development department. It was very stressful, because whenever the manager was at work, I felt like their eyes were always on me, which made it difficult to focus on my work. After a while I noticed that my manager was seated in a nice spot, hidden from the department manager and from pretty much everyone else.

Another situation that I recall was at a work location where they just didn't have enough cubicles for everyone, and I was placed at a desk that had nothing around it. What made it even worse was that there was a large window nearby that had no shades on it and the morning sun would shine in my face for at several hours every day. Needless to say, it was a very uncomfortable location to try and get work done.

Lessons Learned

If you are the new person at a work location, don't be surprised if you are placed in a very uncomfortable position that makes it difficult for you to concentrate and focus on your work. There's probably not much you can do about it until someone else leaves the company and, if you are lucky, you might be able to move into their location.

Difficult to Code or to Use

It's important to distinguish between a software application feature that is difficult to code, and difficult to use. A certain feature could be very easy to develop, but very difficult for people to use. In contrast, a certain feature could be very difficult to code, but very easy for people to use. There are two more combinations of difficulty of coding and difficulty of use, which I will leave as an exercise for you to figure out.

When it comes to developing new features for users of software applications, telling your boss that a certain proposed feature is difficult to code usually is not going to get a warm reception. The users of your application don't care how much work you as a software engineer had to exert in order to implement that feature.

One thing that should be considered when trying to decide whether to implement a particular feature, is how difficult it will be to maintain the coding. If the only way that the code can be written in order to implement the desired functionality will result in code that is hard to maintain in the future, then perhaps a slight modification of the feature should be considered. But in general, nobody cares how much work you have to do as a software engineer in order to get some new functionality working.

Disaster and Recovery

Natural disasters used to be more of a problem than they are today. Before the advent of cloud computing, a typical company's data and applications ran on one or more servers connected via one or more local area networks, and all of the servers and networks were stored in one location. This configuration exposed a company's computer infrastructure to a high level of risk. If a natural disaster, such as a fire or flood, occurred and destroyed a data center, the company's operations would be impacted in a big way.

In the past, preparation for natural disasters emphasized having a backup system available on a moment's notice if needed. The problem with this approach was that if the disaster was large enough, and it affected a large enough number of companies at the same time, then the capacity of any disaster recovery facilities would be overwhelmed and not all of the companies could switch over to the backup systems.

Cloud computing has alleviated this problem to a large extent. The number of locations is so large, and the capacity for redundancy and automatic rollover to backup facilities is so great nowadays, that natural disasters are not the problem that they used to be.

Other types of problems are more likely now, such as hackers breaking into software applications and databases. Instead of preparing for natural disasters, companies and the software engineers who work on their applications need to prepare for other types of disasters and have a way to recover from them.

Efficiency

One of the most important aspects of any software application is efficiency. There is a limited amount of time in each day, and computer programs normally need to produce results as fast as possible. Whenever you tackle an assignment to develop a new application, or a new feature for an existing application, you should consider how to make the code run as quickly as possible. Of course, reliability is also very important. However, there are instances where precise results are not mandatory, and approximations are acceptable. But regardless whether exact answers are needed or approximations are acceptable, getting the results as fast as possible is almost always a top priority.

One of the things that many software engineers fail to include in their designs is planning for potentially huge success of the application. If you design your application assuming that there will be hundreds of users and over time there are millions of users, will your application be able to handle so many users?

Lessons Learned

Considering the efficiency of your software is a good habit to develop. And the best time to do that is when you are in the early design phases of your applications.

Exercise

When you are at the beginning of a project, look for things that will tend to get slower as the size of your database, or the number of users gets larger. How will your software behave as the amount of data or number of users grows? Will you need to completely redesign your application at some point?

Encrypted Laptops

One thing that you have to watch out for is a laptop that has the entire disk drive encrypted for security purposes. Some companies encrypt their laptops is so that if a laptop is lost or stolen, the data stored on the disk drive will be unreadable by anyone other than the legitimate user.

However, there is a serious drawbacks to this approach. I experienced this drawback once with a Windows laptop that had an encrypted hard drive. Sometimes the operating system can hang, making the laptop totally unresponsive to any user commands or keystrokes. In such situations the only action you can take is to force a power shutdown, and then try to turn the power back on.

The problem is that in rare instances, the operating system can become corrupted and the laptop will become totally unusable if you power down the laptop because of the encrypted hard drive. In such cases, the only way to make the laptop usable again is to reformat the hard drive and reinstall the operating system.

Lessons Learned

The potential danger of losing all of the data on your laptop because of an encrypted hard drive is a great reason to make regular backups of your data. You never know when this problem might happen and it's best to be prepared.

Ending a Job

There comes a time in every, or almost every, software engineer's career when it's better to quit your job and move on, rather than stay in your current job. There are many books and articles that discuss this topic, so I'll try to add my unique perspective based on my actual experience, as opposed to just repeating what you can find in those books and articles.

I remember when I was working at AT&T Bell Labs, people used to say that if you stayed at Bell Labs for more than five years you were probably a *lifer*. In other words, it was very unlikely at that point that you would want to leave the comfortable environment of a reasonably well-paying job at a solid company and take your chances going to work somewhere else. Switching jobs and companies involves a certain degree of risk, and it seemed to me that the people who worked at Bell Labs, when I worked there, tended to be risk-averse when it came to their jobs. And why not? A job at the old AT&T Bell Labs was very secure, assuming that you didn't make any major political mistakes and you kept producing good results year after year.

One of the things that I used to hear from people was that once you announce to your employer that you are going to be leaving, if the company makes you a counteroffer in order to make you change your mind and stay, then you should never accept such a counteroffer. I always followed that advice and it seems to have worked out well for me.

I remember one job where I could tell that things were not going so well. I wasn't enjoying the work, my boss seemed to be less than enthusiastic about my performance, and I had started looking around for another job. Once I found it, and I had an offer in hand which I had accepted, I scheduled a short meeting with my manager to tell him that I was planning to resign and move on in my career. At the meeting, I told him my plans, and I handed him my formal resignation letter. To my surprise, he pulled out from his desk drawer a letter of his own which he told me he was planning to hand to me later that same day, to officially let me go from my position at the company. It was a surreal experience. Looking back on it, that was one of the few times that my boss and I were both thinking the same way! It's a shame that we didn't think the same way more often when it came to the actual work that we were doing. It would have made the job much more enjoyable.

There are many reasons why a company might decide to lay a whole group of people off. And there are many terms used by different companies to refer to the same process. Over time, the words that companies have used to mean letting people go have included the following: firing, letting go, reduction of headcount, downsizing, rightsizing, and several others.

The reasons why a company might decide to reduce its headcount include these:

• Financial results in general were poor, and the company needs to reduce expenses

• The company regularly lays off a certain percentage of its staff every year to eliminate the worst performing employees

• A specific division of the company has been losing money and the company wants to totally eliminate it

Regardless of the reason why a company might decide to

reduce its staff, as a software engineer it's in your best interest to be aware of the layoff history at all of the companies that you might be interested in joining at some point in your career. For example, if a company is known to have a history of laying off some percentage of its workforce regularly, for whatever reason, you might want to factor that into your decision process when you are looking for a job. If the way that a company decides who to eliminate is not based totally on the job performance of the individual, and you are a very good or excellent performer in your field, then you will be taking a larger risk by joining one of those companies.

One thing that I think is very important, and unfortunately many companies don't do this very well, or even do it at all, is conducting an exit interview. This is a special kind of interview that the company does when an employee leaves, whether it is because the employee resigned or was let go. The exit interview is an valuable opportunity for a company to find out what went wrong, assuming that the employee is quitting, and for the employee to learn more about why they are being terminated.

Lessons Learned

Regularly changing jobs, whether it's because you want a change or because your employer isn't happy with your work for whatever reason, is just a fact of life for many software engineers. The best thing to do is to always be thinking what your next job might be after your current job ends. That way, you will be better prepared to move on when the time comes.

Estimating

One of the most important skills that a software engineer needs to have, and one which is commonly overlooked, is the ability to accurately estimate the effort needed to perform the coding and testing of any part of a project. Good project managers will ask the software engineers on their teams for estimates, rather than relying on their own experience as project managers.

One of the most interesting approaches for estimating that I've seen in my career involved using a software estimating tool that had a database of coding effort data collected from real projects at real companies. After entering a project's list of tasks and the skill level of the software engineers assigned to each task, the tool estimated time and cost by using the data in its database.

The best estimates are usually obtained by breaking a project down into a collection of tasks, estimating each of the tasks, and adding up the numbers to arrive at a total estimate for the project. The larger the number of tasks and the smaller each task is, the easier it is to do estimation.

My experience has been that keeping accurate records of a team's performance and comparing it with the original estimates at the end of each task is extremely helpful. Doing so will help point out which estimates were too high, too low, or right on target, and will help make future estimates more accurate.

Lessons Learned

It's important to keep track of your own work as you gain experience on real projects, so that you will be able to provide accurate estimates to project managers and others in management.

Fads

Throughout my career I've noticed certain new ideas in computer programming become very popular for short periods of time, and then lose interest among software engineers when a better idea come along. Sometimes, however, these *fads* end up becoming essential tools in computer programmer toolkits.

An example of the former is the EJB technology which is a method for invoking software remotely over a network and was invented in the late 1990's. I remember learning EJB quickly in order to work on a project that used EJB. Other methods have since become much more popular for new development, but a lot of code running today still uses EJB.

An example of the latter is the idea of *Design Patterns*, which suddenly became popular with the publication in 1994 of the book "Design Patterns" by the four authors Gamma, Helm, Johnson, and Vlissides. Hype galore relating to design patterns continued for years after the book was published. I attended a conference about object oriented programming and there were booths with companies touting their products that would help programmers implement the design patterns. Even today it's selling very well online. Since then, design patterns have just become another tool in the profession software engineer's toolkit without the fanfare.

Lessons Learned

It's hard to tell which technologies will be short-term fads and which ones will remain popular with programmers for many years. Instead of trying to determine which is which, it's best to learn at least something about all new technologies as they arise. One of them might keep you employed for longer than you think.

Financial Incentives

Over the course of my career, I have seen various financial incentives offered by companies to encourage candidates to apply for a position, and to keep employees happy while on the job so that they are less likely to want to go somewhere else.

In my opinion, the salary a company offers is the most important financial incentive and a 401(k) plan with a good matching percentage and a relatively quick vesting period is the second most important.

One of the incentives commonly offered by startups is equity in the company. If the company does well and goes public, you might be able to cash in your equity shares at some point. My experience has been that the likelihood of converting equity to cash is fairly low. Whenever I was offered this kind of incentive, I always gave it a low priority on my list of decision factors.

Another incentive is the ability to buy shares of company stock at a discount. This is typically done at public companies who have stock that trades on one of the stock exchanges. The advice I used to hear was to limit investing in the stock of the company you work for, because if the company does poorly financially, not only will the stock decrease in value, but the chances of being laid off increase.

Lessons Learned

When evaluating the financial aspects of a job, I have found it most useful to focus primarily on salary and the 401(k) plan, and ignore other incentives like bonuses. Salaries are usually secure, but bonuses are normally not guaranteed.

First Impressions

There's a common saying that goes something like "You only have one opportunity to make a first impression." And it's true. You need to be careful when you first meet someone because you can't undo what you say or do during that first encounter.

Now, think about what happens when you visit a company for the first time during an in-person job interview. I'm probably dating myself here, since nowadays many in-person job interviews are done remotely using some sort of video conferencing system.

Assuming that you are able to visit the company location where you will most likely work once you get a job, your visit allows you to get a first impression of the company. If you are able to do an in-person interview at the company office, there are many aspects of the first impression that you have of the company to consider. You should pay attention to the building, offices, cubicles and open spaces, cafeteria, parking, safety features, the people you meet, and the general feeling you get when walking around the inside of the workspace.

Lessons Learned

When you are going on an in-person interview, remember that not only will you be making first impressions on the people who will interview you, but they will be making first impressions on you. An in-person interview is your chance to see a company up close, so don't waste the opportunity to gather as much information about the people and operations of the company as you can while you are there.

Foul Language and Fist Banging

Every now and then, I would join a project or a team that had one or more members who used a lot of foul language when talking. It made no difference whether they were speaking casually in the coffee room or hallway, or expressing their opinions formally at a business meeting. Managers never said anything, and colleagues almost never said anything, so those people just kept doing it.

Another thing that I noticed some people do was bang their fists on their desk whenever something happened or someone said something that they didn't like. Again, no manager ever stepped in and said or did anything about this aberrant behavior. Foul language and fist banging don't make for a comfortable work environment. If you have these kinds of tendencies, my suggestion is to sign up for a mixed martial arts class and take out your aggressions there, outside the office. But please don't do that at work.

Lessons Learned

If you are accustomed to using foul language and banging your fists on things at the office, you may be alienating a lot of people without realizing it. The people you work with might not say anything directly to you about it, but that doesn't mean that they aren't affected negatively by it.

Fun, Games, and Food

It's important to have some fun at work. In addition to all of the fun you are having writing code, that is! The kind of fun that people have at programming jobs has evolved over the years. I remember in the 1980's and 1990's people would say "work hard, play hard", which meant that you should work hard at your job, but at the same time make sure that you exert yourself when having fun. I suppose that meant that if you liked to read novels while lounging on a beach chair at the shore, you weren't playing hard enough.

A related phrase that became popular is "work smarter, not harder." If that's true, then does that imply that we should also "play smarter, not harder"? And what would that mean? Perhaps it could mean that it's good to engage in games that exercise your brain, like chess, rather than physical games that can cause you to dislocate a finger, like basketball. I've never heard of anyone dislocating a finger while playing chess on the computer, although I suppose it's possible if you get emotional enough and start banging your fists on your desk in response to losing a piece to the computer chess program.

Eventually, companies realized that it's more efficient if their employees have energetic fun while at the office, so that they will end up spending more time there and presumably getting more work done. This gave rise to the ping pong tables and foosball tables in almost every high-tech startup. It was actually a way of luring prospective new employees to consider joining the company. Of course, free snacks were provided in great quantities since you needed extra energy to work hard on your programming project and play hard at the ping pong table.

I worked on one project at the client's office where there were lots of free snacks and food. In fact, the company brought in professional nutritionists to make sure that the snacks and food were relatively healthy. I'm sure all of those snacks and food made their employees feel good, but must have cost a lot. Unfortunately, due to various cost cutting measures, many companies have reduced their free snacks or eliminated them entirely.

Lessons Learned

Fun, games, snacks, and food are great if a company can afford them. But given the trend of companies trying to do more with less, the amount of free food and other in-office goodies will probably continue to decline. If you expect to see all of those things at the office, you'll probably be disappointed.

Getting Along

When I was starting out in my career, and for many years after that, I tended to take things very seriously. If fact, I probably took things too seriously. One thing that I wasn't prepared for, and which I didn't recognize when it was happening, was when my colleagues would joke around, and poke fun at me, albeit in a friendly way. I should have realized that they were just trying to be friendly, and instead I took it too personally.

I remember hearing about a college football player who had joined a major professional football team. He also took his job a little too seriously. When his teammates tried to poke some fun at him on a plane flight, he got mad at them. One of them pointed out to him that he was in the real world of professional football now, and he could lighten up a bit, especially with his teammates. Once he realized that his teammates were actually trying to help him relax and enjoy the new phase in his football career, he did lighten up and it made his job much more enjoyable.

Lessons Learned

Once you graduate from college and start working in the corporate world, realize that if someone sounds like they are making fun of you, it's probably because they are trying to be friendly and establish a relationship with you. It's not a good idea to take people's comments too seriously. Especially if the context is a casual conversation outside of any formal meetings or business discussions. Given all of the stress that comes with many software engineering jobs, being able to lighten up and joke a little bit with your colleagues can be helpful.

Getting Good at What You Do

One of the things that it is important to realize in the computer software field is that no matter how much you keep learning the latest technology, your skills will gradually become outdated and eventually obsolete. So, the question you need to ask yourself is, "Am I going to be happy continuously learning new skills and techniques, just to see them become obsolete within a few years?" If you want to devote yourself to learning the body of knowledge in a certain field, and not have all of that knowledge become almost worthless in a short period of time, then becoming a software engineer is probably not the best career choice for you.

I enjoyed working in the computer software field for over forty years because I enjoyed working on many different kinds of projects, in different industries and using different languages. But I also found myself getting frustrated because it was hard to just get good at something and enjoy doing the work. There was always the pressure and tension of knowing that in a little while my skills would become more or less obsolete, and I would have to learn a new way of doing essentially the same thing all over again.

Lessons Learned

The software field tends to be one that changes so much and so quickly that it's almost impossible to get good at a particular language or technology and keep doing that for many years. A few notable exceptions are the Java programming language, which has been around since the 1990's, and cloud computing, which seems like it will be with us for many years to come.

Getting the Necessary Experience

There is a sequence of events that seem to happen over and over again in a software engineer's career. What happens is that a new technology becomes available, or perhaps there is a significant improvement in some existing technology that requires new understanding of how it works, and there is suddenly a strong demand for software engineers to work on projects using that new technology. Take the latest hot technology for example, Generative AI tools.

What happens next is that companies start advertising for jobs that require three to five years of experience with that new technology, even though the technology has only around for a year or two. It can be extremely frustrating being in these kinds of situations. I think that the people who succeed the best are those who are continually learning new software technologies as they come into existence.

Lessons Learned

It's impossible to get more years of experience with a relatively new technology than it's been in existence, so you need to do the next best thing which is to keep learning and improving your skills. When it comes to the demands that companies have for people with more experience than is realistically possible, I've found that a good approach is to show how your existing experience can help you get up to speed very quickly on any new technology.

Hidden Code

There are many software tools available that make the life of a software engineer easier, in the sense that if you use those tools then you will end up writing fewer lines of code. How do they accomplish this feat? The simple answer is that they generate "hidden code" that does the actual work of the software application. The hidden code usually lets the programmer think at a higher level of abstraction, without writing all of the lines of code that are needed to implement the functionality that is required.

There are downsides to using these tools, however. For one thing, they generate code that is difficult to see, since the code is purposely hidden from view, and is difficult to unhide in order to see it. Furthermore, once it is revealed, the code that is generated can be very difficult to read and understand. It's generally not formatted very nicely, and it isn't intended to be read by human beings on a regular basis.

Assuming that the code does what you expect, which can be verified by creating a set of test cases and running them successfully, then you normally would never need to look at it. However, when the code does not do what you expect, then you need to start digging up the hidden, generated code and try to understand what it is doing. This can add a lot of time to a software development project. When everything works well, with no issues, then these tools are great time-savers. But when things go wrong, they can turn an on-time, under-budget project into an expensive and lengthy nightmare.

Lessons Learned

If you are thinking about using a software tool or framework, check to see whether it relies on generating hidden code. If it does, and you decide that you want to use that tool or framework anyway, include time and money in your project budget to diagnose issues that might arise with the hidden code.

Holiday Parties

The holiday party is a tradition at many companies. It has its good side, and it has its bad side. In some companies it's required for employees to attend, at other companies it's suggested that employees attend, and at other companies it's totally optional and nobody will wonder why you aren't there. But in all cases, you need to be careful if you decide to attend a company holiday party. It has the ability to help your career, however it also has the ability to hurt your career.

Holiday parties tend to be held in the month of December, to give employees an opportunity to celebrate the year that is almost over, and to do so amongst colleagues and acquaintances. The problem with many of these events is that people tend to forget that they are professionals and they act unprofessionally. Don't allow yourself to fall into that trap.

Lessons Learned

Have fun at company holiday parties, but be careful that you don't act too casually or do something that you will regret later.

Industry Analysis

There are many industries that need to hire computer software engineers. When you are looking for a job, it's important to understand the differences between industries and how those differences can affect your day-to-day work and your long-term career.

One way to analyze the industries that exist is to divide them into three categories: Technical, Moderately Technical, and Non-Technical. In my mind, the Technical industries are the ones consist of companies whose main product or service is highly technical in nature. For example, companies in the areas of telecommunications, computer hardware and software development, and companies that provide computer consulting services and allow other companies to outsource their internal data management requirements.

Moderately Technical industries consist of companies that produce products or provide services that are highly technologically based. For example, the financial companies who need to store and process very large amounts of financial data.

In my opinion, the Non-Technical industries consist of companies whose main products and services do not involve or require a large amount of sophisticated computer software or hardware to produce their products and services. For example, lawn care services, garbage collection services, and so on. They still need to track some information like client lists and some basic financial information, but it's not the same as the others.

All companies require the use of software to track their own internal financial data, email, human resources data, and so on.

However, either all of almost all of those things can be outsourced to third party companies that specialize in storing and processing those kinds of data, and I consider those companies that provide the outsourced services as Highly Technical companies.

Now, the question that we need to consider is what difference, if any, does it make what kind of industry you are working in as a software engineer. In my experience, the companies that value their technical talent the highest are the Technical companies. The Moderately Technical value technical talent to a lesser degree. And the Non-Technical companies value technical talent the least.

Lessons Learned

If you are looking for an environment that is very sophisticated in their use of technology and value your talents the most, I would focus on the Technical Companies. If there is a field of business, such as businesses that store huge amounts of data and need to analyze that data in order to run their business efficiently, then you could also consider Moderately Technical companies. Of course, there are exceptions and you should keep an open mind when exploring companies within different industries.

Inspiration

I developed an interest in computer programming at an early age. Such a statement might seem trite in today's world in which most children are exposed to computer programming in school. At that time, however, during the late 1960's and early 1970's, it was not that common for children or young adults to be interested in computer programming or to even know what it was.

Very few personal computers existed in people's homes for children to experiment with, and there was a lack of educational material in elementary schools related to computer programming. Nowadays, of course, things have changed so much that it's common for children to be interested in, and quite good at, writing software.

One of the first books I can remember reading as a child that caused me to become interested in computers in general, and about the power of computer software in particular, contained a sample program written in the FORTRAN programming language. It's purpose was to calculate the position of train tracks that allow a train to switch from one line to another. It calculated curves using mathematical formulas. The program generated a drawing of the straight train tracks and the curved tracks that connected them together in a gradual way.

The connecting tracks need to change their direction in a gradual way, so that the train won't derail during the process of changing tracks. Mathematical formulas using the Sine and Cosine functions can be used to generate smooth curves that start changing direction very slowly, then accelerate toward the middle of the connecting tracks, and then merge into the other set of tracks at a slowing pace, as you can see in this diagram:

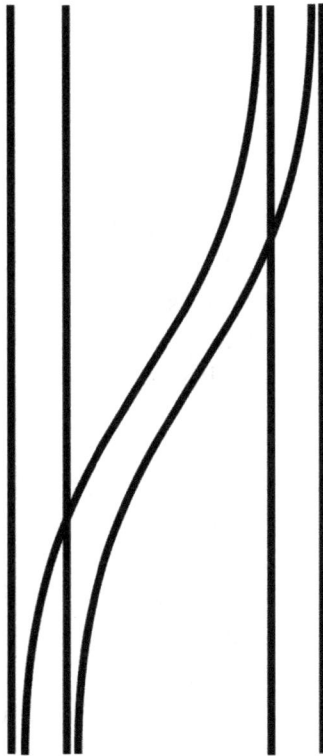

The program basically consisted of a loop where the X and Y coordinates of the curves being drawn would be incremented in the correct direction using the values calculated by the Sine and Cosine functions. Every time the program ran through the loop, another set of points would be drawn on the output printing device. And by connecting all of the points you would see the shape of the connecting tracks. It was a very simple application of some basic mathematical functions, but it was very effective and obviously very useful in real life. It made a very powerful impression on me.

I remember owning, as a young child, a small plastic toy that contained lot of moving parts, and which functioned as a very simple calculating device. It was a kind of "mechanical adding machine". The toy had a few cylindrically shaped "columns" of moving parts, with little bumps on them. Each column represented a digit in a number. The columns of moving parts were connected to each other in a row by other parts. You used a special piece of plastic to indicate a single-digit value that you wanted to add to the main number, and by rotating the columns the toy would somehow calculate the correct answer. I was fascinated by the idea that you could create a mechanical device that would take numbers and perform some arithmetic operations on them. I somehow lost track of that toy, and I've never seen a used one advertised anywhere online, but it was one of my favorite toys.

When I was a little older, I remember visiting the lobby of the IBM building in midtown Manhattan which had a special interactive computer exhibit, and I remember having fun playing with it. The exhibit consisted of a number of text screens, each with its own keyboard, probably connected to an IBM mainframe computer behind the scenes. The computer was running a very early form of artificial intelligence software that mimicked a human being. It would ask you a question, which you could answer by typing on the keyboard. Then, it would ask a follow up question based on your response to the first question. Perhaps it was running the old ELIZA program that had been created at

MIT. It was really amazing to be able to interact with a computer as though it was a real person. Of course, you could tell that it really was not as intelligent as a person—at least I could—and it was fun to try to ask questions that would make the program return funny sounding responses.

This may have been the first time that I had fun trying to get a piece of computer software to do something that it was not originally intended to do. One way to tell how much you love computer programming is whether or not you like to try to make the software crash, or make it do weird things, and then try to figure out how to prevent someone from doing the same thing.

Lessons Learned

Finding things that inspire you about using or developing software will help motivate you to spend the time needed to learn the technology and keep you motivated to learn more as you progress through your career.

Internet of Things–IoT

If you asked most people what the data that is flowing through the Internet primarily consists of, they will probably say that it is web browser data, text messages, and email messages. And that is a very large part of the data that travels on the Internet. However, there is also a very large quantity of data that most people are not aware of, and that is the data that is called IoT data, or Internet of Things data.

It is hidden in a sense, because the IoT data is generated by sensors that are attached to all sorts of physical devices, and is sent silently over the Internet to servers that are constantly receiving and processing the data. The devices can include wearable medical sensors for patients, electronic automobile sensors, and sensors connected to factory machinery, among others.

The term that is used to refer to the data itself is *telemetry* data. Examples of the types of things that can have sensors attached that will send telemetry data to a monitoring server include manufacturing machinery, wearable medical devices, and vehicles.

One of the major issues with IoT data is that most of it is unencrypted. This poses a major risk for companies whose raw telemetry data is flowing unprotected over the Internet.

Lessons Learned

If you want to work on software projects that involved huge quantities of data that originate from electronic sensors, you should look into projects that involved IoT data.

Interviews

Over the years, I was interviewed numerous times for many job opportunities. Many of those interviews went well, and many of them did not go well. The following are descriptions of some of my job interview experiences, and the outcomes, so that you can learn from my successes and my mistakes.

The Phone Screen

One of the most common ways that either a headhunter or a company manager or human resources professional will start the interview process is with a phone screen interview. If you are currently working, finding a private area to talk can pose some challenges.

While I was working in midtown Manhattan, I would go to the Port Authority Bus Terminal and sit in one of the coffee shops to take a call from a headhunter. The price of a small cup of coffee seemed worth it to me to be able to sit in a relatively quiet area, for midtown Manhattan that is.

Another place that I would go in Manhattan was the bookstore that used to be in the McGraw Hill building. It had lots of technical computer books on display, so in addition to being able to take a phone call in a relatively quiet area, I had fun browsing through all of the books.

Lessons Learned

Wherever your current job is located, try to find one or more quiet places that you can easily get to on your lunch break to take phone calls. If you are able to combine taking the phone call with doing something enjoyable, so much the better.

Know Your Laptops

Some of the worst experiences I had on in-person interviews were when I was asked to write some code, and was provided a laptop that I was not familiar with. Specifically, I had used a Microsoft Windows laptop for many years, and I didn't have experience using an Apple Macintosh laptop. There are some significant differences between the special keys on the keyboards of these two brands of laptop, and if you are not familiar with those differences and don't have experience using them, then you will have trouble in a technical interview.

Lessons Learned

Make sure that you are familiar with, and comfortable using, a Macintosh laptop as well as a Windows laptop. There are subtle differences between the two, especially when it comes to typing certain important key combinations. If you are asked to write some code at an interview with a laptop that you are not familiar with using, that could derail the whole interview and cause you to lose the job opportunity.

The Good

In-person interviews that continue past the scheduled end time usually go well. Busy managers are not prone to spending unnecessary time with people or things that they are not interested in. The length of an interview is not always reliable, but it tends to be a good indicator. Interviews that went well for me included those where I arrived on time, was relaxed, and was well-prepared to answer most of the questions that were asked of me.

One interview that went well involved a technical test on the

C programming language. I was told at the end of the interview that I was the only person they had interviewed who had answered all of the questions on that test correctly. I got the job.

The Bad

There was a small startup company that I interviewed with, and the technical part of the interview centered around solving a problem involving random numbers. I was supposed to design an algorithm that would split a range of numbers into four equal groups, where the probability of each number appearing in each group was equal. It was an interesting puzzle, but one that I had not solved before. I did my best to come up with a solution, however my solution didn't quite work perfectly. I explained my reasoning and thought process, and I thought that I had done a good job given the circumstances. After I had spoken with several people on the team, I was told by the manager that they would not be making me an offer. I asked, "Why not?" I was told that since I hadn't fully solved the problem, I had failed the interview. Apparently, for that company, if you couldn't fully solve the problem in the given amount of time, then it really didn't matter how much experience you had, or how you answered any of the other questions.

The interview also included a lot of comments about my age, and whether I would feel comfortable working with people who are much younger than me. Given that it is generally illegal to ask people their age and to discriminate against applicants based on their age, and given that the only thing that seemed to matter to them was whether or not I solved the "puzzle", I wasn't upset to walk out of the building without an offer. I don't think that I would have enjoyed working there anyway.

In another interview, I was asked what I would do in a hypothetical situation where my future boss wanted to take the software design in a certain direction, and I realized that it would be a mistake to go down that path. Would I go along with the boss? Would I object and openly disagree with the boss? How far would I take my objection? Would I risk being fired in order to stand up to the boss and insist that they were making a big mistake? I described one situation that I had experienced on an actual project, and what I told the interviewer was that I objected to the design decision, and I explained my reasoning, but in the end I decided to go with the decision because it seemed to me that it probably didn't make that much difference which way we went with the design. Well, apparently that wasn't the answer that the interviewer was looking for. They told me directly that what I should have done is stood firm in my objection, and refused to go along with my boss. Because of that, they said that they would not be extending a job offer to me.

Another interview I remember very well involved a relatively small financial company that was looking for someone with UNIX experience. In addition to the technical computer experience, the candidate needed to have some familiarity with finance and investing. However, the company was willing to train the person in the financial area. The company was located in a city with a downtown and surrounding suburbs. I was booked into a hotel in one of the suburbs and I had a rental car. On the morning of the interview, which was scheduled to start at 9 a.m., I started driving from the hotel to the job location. I soon realized that most of the other people living in that suburb also were driving into the downtown area for work. Due to the heavy rush-hour traffic, I arrived at the interview about thirty minutes late. During the interview, I was asked about my opinion of corporate bonds.

At the time, I didn't think that bonds were a great investment and I expressed my negative opinion of them. Unfortunately, the company thought that bonds were a very important part of any investment portfolio and they were not happy with my answer.

Lessons Learned

First, when interviewing in a city that you are not familiar with, always leave yourself extra time for delays. Coming late to an interview makes a very bad impression. Second, if the interviewer asks you for your opinion about something relating to the business that the company is engaged in, be very careful when answering. If you are not knowledgeable enough to state opinions about that subject, try to answer in a way that supports whatever the company's approach is.

The Strange

One of the interviews that I had seemed to go well, but the end result was no job offer. The company was a consulting company that was trying to get a contract with a large company, and they were interested in me because of my background. Instead of just saying that they were not going to make me an offer, the company kept in touch with me for several months trying to keep me interested in the job until they were ready. Unfortunately, by the time the new role became available, and the consulting company finally contacted me to invite me to join them, I had already found a new project and was no longer interested. It would have been much better for me if they had made a decision and brought me on board sooner rather than later. I fully understand that sometimes a project can't be started because the client is not ready to move forward. However, a company is taking a chance by not making an offer and risking losing the person to another company and project. I suppose that is the nature of consulting companies, and you just have to accept it.

Another interview that had an unexpected outcome was one that I had early in my career with one of the large brokerage companies on Wall Street. They had brought in a group of candidates, since they were looking to hire multiple computer programmers, and I was one of that group. Before the interview, we were all sitting in a room together, and everyone was chatting about their experiences working at some other large brokerage business. Since I had never worked at that kind of company before, I realized that I didn't fit in with the other candidates in the group in terms of previous experience. After my interview was completed, I was told that they had rejected my application. When I asked why, they told me that I seemed to have a very strong mind and that I probably would find the work too simple and not challenging enough. That was certainly not what I was expecting!

Lessons Learned

Always ask why you were rejected for a job after having interviewed in person. The reason that you receive may be very informative and enlightening.

Japan

One of the pieces of advice that I used to hear was that international experience would be good for your career. Based on that advice, I sought out an opportunity that was involved with software in some other part of the world. I landed at a Japanese software technology company with an office in New York City.

The experience was certainly different. I learned some Japanese language, got involved with creating Japanese language versions of various software tools, and I had the opportunity to travel to Tokyo a couple of times.

One of the Japanese technical terms that took me a while to decipher sounded like *Vazhan Appu*. The first word wasn't that hard to guess, since it sounds very much like the English word *version*. But the word that gave me a lot of trouble was the word that sounds like *Appu*. At first I thought that it was a short form of the word *application*, since the Japanese commonly abbreviate multi-syllabic words to make them easier to pronounce. It turns out that the word "Appu" is actually the way that the Japanese pronounce the English word *up*. In this case, the word *up* is actually an abbreviation of the word *upgrade*. So, what the expression *Vazhan Appu* means in English is *version upgrade*. This is actually quite a commonly used term because most software products are upgraded to new versions rather frequently.

Lessons Learned

Working on Japanese software was interesting and a change of pace, but it was outside the mainstream of software development. Before getting involved with foreign software, it's worth evaluating whether it will move your career forward.

Job Hopping

The term job hopping refers to the idea of moving from one company to another in rapid succession. In the past, the general wisdom was that job hopping was not a good thing to do. The reasoning was that if you job hop too frequently, then you won't build up your knowledge and experience within a certain company and industry, in addition to giving the perception that you are not a loyal employee and will jump ship as soon as you discover a better opportunity elsewhere. The people who end up being promoted into positions of increasing responsibility tend to be those who stay with the company for an extended period of time.

One thing that I found when I stayed at a company beyond a period of a few years was that many of the people I worked with ended up moving on to other opportunities. This included coworkers as well as my managers. The problem with this is that all of the effort that I put into building relationships with my coworkers and with my managers would just go to waste when they left the company. It takes time to build trust with a manager, and when that manager leaves the company it means that you have to start all over again establishing a new relationship with a new manager.

Lessons Learned

It's not good to stay at a company so long that all of the people you know have left the company. It should be a sign to you that perhaps it's time for you to also pack up your bags and move on to another job.

Job Location

The place where your job is located can make a big difference, not only on your quality of life outside the office, but also in the office.

I'll give you an example from my experience. One of my jobs was located in the Princeton NJ area. The work location was nice enough, but after I started working there I discovered that most of the people I was working with lived in the Philadelphia area and commuted every day to Princeton. The net effect of this was that I had very little in common with them. They would talk about the Philadelphia sports teams, for example, and they had very little interest in what was going on in New Jersey, and certainly not in New York City. I felt like I was working in a different state.

Lessons Learned

When you are deciding on taking a job in a new geographic area, check whether there are a lot of people who commute there from another state. If so, you could be in for some rough times as far as making new friends at work is concerned.

Job Titles

Are job titles important? Does it matter what your title is? When you are job hunting, should you care what the job title is for the job that you are applying for? I've heard opinions on both sides of the question.

In my opinion, the answer is: it depends. Sometimes the exact job title is important, and sometimes it isn't. A lot of it depends on the specific company you are working for, and how your career progresses.

One thing to keep in mind is that as you progress in your career as a computer software developer, the jobs that you held in the past will be listed on your resume along with the job titles. So, to a certain extent, your current job title will become a reference point for job recruiters in the future to help them determine what level of candidate you are. If all of your job titles have the word Senior in them, then it indicates a higher level, everything else being equal, than someone who has the word Junior in their job titles. Similarly, if you never have a job title with the word *Architect* in it, then recruiters may wonder whether or not you have sufficient architecture experience for the job they are trying to fill.

You might think that since a software architect is a higher level position than a software engineer, having a job title of software architect on your resume would be a positive thing. However, in my experience the exact opposite can happen. Some companies feel that architects are not hands-on enough, and they doubt whether a person who has worked as a software architect could write code as well as a software engineer could.

Job titles can have special meaning within different companies. For example, one company I landed a job with offered me a position with a title of *Advanced Software Engineer*. The title sounded good, so I didn't think that much about the fact that the job title didn't have the word *Senior* in it. After I started the job I discovered that the job title *Advanced Software Engineer* actually indicated a lower level than the title *Senior Software Engineer*, and the two job titles had different pay ranges defined for them. Since my starting salary was at the top end of the pay range for the Advanced Software Engineer title, in order to get a pay raise I had to work very hard to get promoted to Senior Software Engineer. Looking back on it, I should have asked what the different job titles were in the company before accepting an offer. I could have saved myself a lot of headaches.

Lessons Learned

It can be tempting to ignore the specifics of your job title, especially when looking for a new position. But your exact job title can be very important, both for your new position within the company and how you will be perceived in the future when companies look at your resume.

Knowing Too Much

Is there such a thing as knowing too much about software? There might be, depending on your own personal mindset when it comes to learning and growing. Let me explain.

I think that there were a couple of things about software development that attracted me in the first place. One was the opportunity to keep learning new things, with the result being that work doesn't get boring. If you get very good at doing some kind of work, but the work itself rarely changes, it can become very boring. If you are the kind of person who likes to be challenged to learn new things, then doing the same thing over and over will probably make you unhappy in the long run.

The other was the ever-increasing market for programming talent as new technologies are introduced. This almost guarantees that software developers who are willing to put in the effort to keep growing will continue to have employment opportunities for many years.

Now, how does this relate to "knowing too much"? What I found during my career was that I enjoyed the process of learning and using new technologies because it kept things interesting. But I was afraid that if I learned a certain technology too well, to the point where there wasn't much new to learn about that particular technology, then it would become boring. So, I tended to hold back and not learn everything that there was to know about any particular technology in order to keep the excitement going as I gradually learned new facets of each technology.

The other thing that I was afraid of was becoming too much of an expert at something, and then getting pigeon-holed into that technology. Sort of like an actor who becomes known for one type of role, and is very successful at it, and then has a hard time breaking into any other types of roles because they have become synonymous with the role that they became famous for.

Looking back on it, with 20/20 hindsight, I think that it would have been better not to worry about how much of an expert I became in any particular technology. And especially now that the software field is changing so rapidly, there really isn't enough time to have the luxury of not learning everything that you can about each software technology. This relates to one of the things that I learned from one of my managers, that you should consider all possible options as much as possible before making a decision. Similarly, when you are using a particular software technology, I think that it is very important to learn about all of the features of that technology, even those that you don't think you might ever need to use, because just knowing about their existence will help you to make better design decisions when creating the software that you are assigned on a project.

Lessons Learned

It is important to try to learn as much as you can about the technology that you are currently using, as well as any other technologies that relate to it and could become more useful alternatives at some point in the future. It's better to keep learning as much as possible, and not to worry about whether you will get bored, or get pigeon-holed.

Lazy Software

Over the years, software has become lazy. What does that mean? The basic idea is that there are many times within a software application that certain actions don't have to be done immediately. Instead, the action can be put off until there is an actual need for the action.

For example, let's say your software program needs to initialize some data before you can execute a certain task. And let's say that there are twenty such initializations that need to be done. But each initialization only needs to be done if the user will do something specific that requires that data to be initialized. It would be inefficient to do all twenty data initializations if the user is only planning to do five of the twenty things.

The solution is to only do each initialization at the time that the user makes a specific request that requires that particular data initialization. There are many software programming languages and related tools that use this approach to speed up operations. If you read the literature, you'll see terms like "lazy loading", which means that one or more data values aren't loaded into a computer program until the software actually needs to use them.

Of course, there are potential pitfalls with this lazy approach. For example, if the data changes over time, and you need to load the data into your program as it existed at a particular point in time, then lazy loading of that data would not give you the results that you want because the data would be too old by the time it gets loaded into your program. Perhaps deciding whether or not to use lazy loading is an example of a task that human computer programmers can do better than artificial intelligence software.

95

Learning a New Codebase

One of the most difficult things that I have had to do as a professional software engineer is to quickly learn how an existing set of code works. Unless you join a project at the very beginning of the development of a totally new system, which very rarely happens, you will have to be able to quickly understand the inner working of a large amount of existing code that other people have written.

Various tools have been developed over the years to help programmers understand existing code, and it's a worthwhile investment of your time to become familiar with as many of these tools as you can.

Lessons Learned

The more code you look at that you are not familiar with, the better you will get at doing it.

Exercise

Once in a while, take a new set of code that you have not worked with before, such as the code for a tool that is stored in a public online repository like GitHub, and try to understand how it works. Perhaps this exercise would be a fun thing to do at a brown bag meeting with other software engineers. See the section titled *Lunch and Learn* if you don't know what a brown bag session is.

Limiting Questions

I joined a team once that was using a variety of technologies that I was not familiar with. It was a challenge getting up to speed quickly not only on the technologies that were new to me, but also the business aspects of the application. In order to do my job, I needed to learn a lot of information in a hurry. Unfortunately, in these types of situations there often isn't someone, like a mentor, to whom you can turn for answers.

I remember asking one of the members on that team a few questions one day, and then all of a sudden that person stopped answering my questions, and started ignoring me. When I mentioned this to my boss, his response was "Well, you must have reached the question limit for that person today. Try again tomorrow."

It can be frustrating not being able to get answers to questions, however I've learned that there really are limits to how many questions the average team member can answers each day. Especially if there is a time crunch and everyone on the project is working hard to achieve some goal by a certain date.

It would be best if any new team member were assigned a mentor to help get them up to speed as quickly as possible. However, this is sometimes a luxury that companies and projects cannot afford. When you find yourself in these kinds of situations, you need to get creative in finding ways to get answers to your questions.

If you happen to be that person on the team who knows the answers, and someone else is the new person who expects you to answer their questions whenever they ask, I suggest that you tell the other person in a nice way that you are really busy now, and could they come back tomorrow, rather than just ignoring them. Or perhaps try to point them in the right direction so that they can figure out the answer themselves. A few kind words will help maintain good relationships within the team and help keep everyone focused on getting the work done as a team.

Lessons Learned

Asking other members of your team about the code that you need to work on can become annoying to those members. Be mindful of their time, and try to answer your questions as well as you can by yourself first. If you must ask others for help understanding something, try to spread your questions around among the members of your team and don't ask too many questions on the same day.

Local Experts and How to Deal With Them

At some point in your software engineering career, you will probably encounter someone a local "expert" on some software technology. That person might also be the system administrator of the software application or system. The problem that sometimes arises is that the expert might not want anyone else to become as much of an expert as they are, so that they can have more job security. And they might want to control all of the software settings, such as security levels and system functionality.

I've been in situations like this in my career, and it's not fun when someone feels that they need to have a tight control over what anyone can do on their system. Sometimes it's necessary for security reasons to restrict people's access or abilities to do various things in the system. But every now and then someone just wants to exert their control over other people, and thinks that they need to do so in order to keep their job. Management should be aware of these situations and act accordingly to prevent people from getting too frustrated and then wanting to leave the project or company for another place to work.

Lessons Learned

In any job, you should try to quickly identify who are the local experts, and system administrators, within your department and/or project. And you should try to become friendly with them, so that they will be willing to help you when you are in a bind and need some speedy assistance. It's not always easy to do, but you need to try. If you are a manager, you should keep an eye out for system administrators who are power hungry and enjoy restricting software engineers unnecessarily.

99

Long Lasting Programming Languages

There are certain programming languages that have grown tremendously in popularity during last few decades and have maintained their position as leading languages in the software development field. Why do some languages becomes bright stars and others fade away into obscurity? And how can you detect new languages that will become stars and on which you can build a career in software development?

Let's take a look at a couple of them—one which I worked with almost from the beginning of its existence and worked with for most of my lengthy career and another one which I worked with a lot toward the end of my career.

The first one is the Java programming language. It was first introduced to the world in the mid 1990's and is still going strong. When it first was released it was intended as a specialized language for ancient devices call "set-top boxes", those cable boxes that people used to put on top of their television sets. People realized relatively quickly that the language had a lot of nice features that made it very useful as an object-oriented programming language (OOPL) without the drawbacks of other OOPLs that were available at the time. Corporate sponsorship of the language, first by Sun Microsystems and later by Oracle helped strengthen Java in the language marketplace. Since its initial versions, Java has been enhanced many times to keep it current with general programming practices within the software industry, such as the features of *functional programming*. Because of all of the patches that have been added onto Java over the years which have made the language become somewhat clunky, a new language called Kotlin was developed to address many of the issues and remain compatible to a large extent with existing Java code.

The other language is the Python programming language which was first released in the early 1990's and is also continuing to grow in popularity. Python brought a slew of new features to programming languages such as the *zip* function that combines or *zippers* together two lists of data. Python is also an interpreted language which means that each line of code is translated into an underlying machine language on the fly and then executed. It's similar to the way that Java is converted first into an intermediate language that is then executed in a special *virtual machine*. This allows the language to run on many platforms and operating systems, just like Java can.

Python has also been evolving since its creation, and underwent a major revamp when version 3.0 was released at the end of the year 2008. Version 3.0 had such significant changes that most code written prior to that version needed to be modified before it would even run using the version 3.0 Python interpreter.

Lessons Learned

There seem to be a few traits that the immensely popular programming languages have in common. First, they bring something new and different to the programming world. Second, they are relatively easy to learn initially and have a lot of depth for developing sophisticated software as one becomes more adept at the language. Third, they can run on many hardware platforms and operating system environments. Fourth, they have strong support from corporate America as well as hobbyists and tinkerers. Fifth, they are continually being enhanced to provide more functionality and ease of use as the needs of professional software engineers change.

Java and Python have all of the above characteristics. Another trait of both Java and Python is their interpreted aspect. Being either partly or completely interpreted rather than exclusively compiled allows them to run in many environments, helping to guarantee their popularity and long lives. If you see a new programming language appear on the market, see whether it is easy to learn, at least partly interpreted, can run on many platforms, and is supported by at least one major software company. If the new language has all of those aspects, it could become your ticket to many years of employment as a software engineer.

Longevity

Several years ago, in the mid-2010s, when I was looking for a new position, a headhunter told me that he was very impressed with how I had kept up with the changing technologies, unlike most other people my age. At that point, I was already in my late 50's. It gets harder to pick up new skills as you get older, so you need to have a very strong desire to keep working at it and keep learning new things. Or, to put it another way, to keep learning all of the new ways to do the same old things. I think this has been one of the major factors in allowing me to stay employed in the software field for so long. I didn't give up, even though it was getting harder to keep up.

Lessons Learned

As you get older, you need to force yourself to keep learning new technical skills. Even though it gets harder as you age, if you want to stay employed in the software field you need to force yourself to keep learning new tools and technologies. Luckily there are many ways to do that, including many online courses, books, blogs and articles. You just need to be willing to allocate time and effort regularly to keep learning.

Exercise

If you are currently not enrolled in any course, either online or in person, pick something to study and enroll in a course on that subject. The important thing is to keep learning and not become stagnant in your development.

Lunch and Learn

If the company that you work for has the budget for lunch and learn sessions, then I highly recommend that you try to arrange for some of these events. Back in the mid-1990's, the Java programming language was just starting to become popular. And it did so very quickly. It was obvious to me that knowing how to program using the Java language was going to be a very important skill that I needed to add to my bag of programming tricks. It also seemed like a great opportunity to get together on a regular basis with my co-workers to learn something new and to get to know my fellow software engineers better

I once suggested to my manager that we hold regular meetings every week to discuss Java. The manager liked the idea and provided refreshments for the attendees in addition to a conference room for us to hold our weekly lunch and learn sessions. If you are not familiar with the term *lunch and learn,* perhaps you've heard some people call these meetings *brown bag* sessions or maybe something else.

Lessons Learned

If there is a hot new technology that a lot of people in your company could benefit from learning about, consider holding regular lunch and learn sessions to create a sense of joint ownership of the learning process. These meetings are also a great way to improve morale among the software engineering staff. If you are lucky, management will pay the costs of refreshments and will give you and your co-workers the time needed to hold the meetings.

Managers

Managers can be very good, very bad, or somewhere in the middle. The managers who stand out in my mind are the ones who, in my opinion, were either very good or very bad.

Good Managers

When you have a good manager, it's a pleasure. You can focus on getting your work done, you have support from your manager, and your manager will handle a lot of the office politics before it has a chance to affect team members. Good managers also encourage you to keep learning and growing, and they are careful about not giving you assignments to do that are way beyond your capabilities.

Bad Managers

I've had managers who had virtually no technical background or training, but who got assigned to be a manager of a technical team of computer programmers. Basically, they were promoted into a managerial role as a reward for doing a good job in some other non-technical area. I remember one day going to get a printout of something from the printer, and my manager criticized me for wasting time using the printer. That same manager also told me that if I wasn't sitting at my desk all day typing on the keyboard, then I wasn't doing a good job. In other words, that manager's metric for determining a good job was the percentage of an employee's time spent each day typing on the keyboard rather than what they actually produced. I truly hope that nobody reading this book ever ends up working for a manger who has no technical background and can't relate to software engineers on their level.

Sometimes you get lucky and get a red flag about a manager before you decide to take the job. The challenge is being able to recognize the red flag when it happens. One time I was walking from my car in the company parking lot to the building for an in-person interview with the hiring manager. On the way into the building, someone said "Hi" to me. They asked me whether I was there for an interview, and I said "Yes". Then, they asked me who I was interviewing with, and when I said the name of the manager the person in the parking lot made a face and said something like "Oh boy, good luck!". Only later, after I started working on the job did I realize that the encounter in the parking lot was a red flag. It's easy to miss these things if you are not paying attention.

Lessons Learned

If you are walking into a building for an interview, watch out for potential red flags from other people who work at that company regarding the manager that you are interviewing with. If you mention the manager by name, and people have a negative reaction, don't dismiss it completely. It could save you from taking a job with a manager that will make your life miserable until you get your next job after that.

Another example of something that one of my managers did that was not good was using phrases from movies when carrying on conversations with employees. It took me a while to catch on and understand what was being said, but eventually I realized that all of those phrases were quotes from various movies that the manager had seen and enjoyed. Unfortunately, I wasn't, and still am not, a big movie watcher, so those phrases didn't resonate with me. In fact, they just sounded strange.

I also realized at some point that one or two of the members of my team were able to relate to all of those phrases, and that caused a division between those team members and me because they had the "inside information" about what the manager was saying and what was implied by those phrases. It made me feel that those other team members were somehow closer to the manager, and perhaps were being treated in a more friendly manner than other employees who didn't share the same tastes in movies.

If you are a software engineer who has taken on leadership responsibilities, try to avoid using phrases from popular movies or TV shows that only a small number of your employees will understand and relate to. Otherwise, you might end up causing those employees who are not familiar with those phrases to feel unwelcome on your team, and it could cause morale issues.

My own experience led me to conclude that there are more bad managers than good managers. If you happen to find yourself as a member of team that is managed by a good manager, consider yourself lucky and don't be in a rush to leave your manager.

Mathematics and Software

How much knowledge of mathematics necessary in order to succeed in a software development career? As I've said in a few other places, it depends.

When I was in college, I studied a lot of mathematics. I estimate that I've used almost none of it in my career as a software engineer. But that's mainly because the kinds of software applications that I worked didn't involve much mathematics.

If I had worked on certain kinds of sophisticated financial software or scientific software, then the level of mathematics involved would have been much greater.

Lessons Learned

Consider what kinds of applications you want to work on as a software engineer. If they are primarily involved with moving data from one place to another, such as gathering streaming IoT data and storing it in a very large database from which various reports and charts will be drawn, then you probably don't need to study much advanced mathematics.

Meaning

Have you ever found yourself wondering why you are doing what you are doing, thinking that what you are doing with your life seems to have no purpose, and hoping that you could do something more "meaningful"? These thoughts probably occur to most people at some point in their careers, and I suspect that they occur especially frequently to software engineers. After all, how meaningful can it be to write statements in some programming language that causes pieces of data to move from one place to another? In fact, that is what much of computer programming is about at its most fundamental level.

To help answer this question, one thing to keep in mind is that by working, and earning a living, you are helping society because you aren't on the receiving end of charity. In fact, one of the greatest forms of charity is to help someone get a job so that they can sustain themselves financially and not need any more charity. Just the fact that you are working and earning a salary is already something that has great meaning, even if you don't realize it.

But working and earning a salary is something that applies to any job, not just a career in computer software. So, the question remains: "How can one find meaning in a career of software development?" To answer this question, let's consider the true story of a professional actor who admitted publicly that he was not happy with his career as an actor because he didn't get involved with the creative side of acting. Meaning that he just did what he was told by the directors: Stand here, look this way or that way, say this, make this facial expression, and so on. But he didn't get an opportunity to get involved with deciding what to say, or how to say it, or what expression to have on his face. This left a gaping hole in his feeling of satisfaction with his career, because he was never given the opportunity to be creative in his profession.

The same idea can be applied to software development, which can potentially involve a great deal of creative activity. If one spends their entire career writing code according to someone else's specifications, and not getting involved with thinking up new ideas for software applications, then one could end up feeling very dissatisfied with their software career, just like that actor felt about his acting career.

Other things that you can do are to think about how the software that you are developing is helping society. Again, this is something that can be applied to many careers, not just software development. Just about everything that anyone does in any career, perhaps with a few exceptions, helps the world in some way or another. I tried to think this way about the software that I was working on when I was involved with the pharmaceutical industry. However, in my experience, I found that if the work itself doesn't offer much opportunity for creativity, the idea that one is helping society often is not enough to overcome a feeling of disappointment in what one is doing on a daily basis.

Lessons Learned

If your career has the potential for you to be creative, and you have a creative side, and you are either not given opportunities or don't aggressively pursue opportunities to apply creativity in your field, then you will probably end up being disappointed in your career. You will feel that all of that time spent working on various projects was just spending time and earning a salary, and not much more.

Meeting People At Work

The Big Boss

I had worked at the company for quite a while before I finally said hello to the director of the whole office. When I had interviewed at the company, he didn't meet me or speak with me. After I started working at the company, I would walk past his office every day on the way to my cubicle, which was not more than twenty feet away. I never said "Hello", and he never said "Hello" to me. One day, after several months of this, I decided that it had been long enough that we had not spoken to each other even once, and I walked into his office and introduced myself. He seemed to know who I was, somehow, and seemed to be a little upset with the fact that we had not spoken until then. But in my mind, it was his responsibility as a senior manager to make the effort to take that first step of introducing himself to me. After all, how could I know when would be a good time to interrupt his busy schedule and make contact?

Lessons Learned

If you are a senior manager who runs an operation in a certain location, you should make it your business to meet all of the members of your staff. At least once when each person starts their job, and probably at least once a year after that. It will help to improve morale within the company, and it will help make employees feel that someone high up in the company cares about them. This could make the difference between someone staying in the company or leaving for another opportunity. And if you are an employee whose upper level management is located near where you sit, make sure to say "Hello" once in a while, especially if the manager tends to stay in their office all the time and never ventures out to talk with people. They might be waiting for you to take that first step, and might judge you negatively if you wait too long to do so.

The System Administrators

If you are lucky enough to work in a company where you can actually get to meet and become friendly with any of the people who administer the various parts of the software and hardware infrastructure that runs the company's software applications, consider it a special gift and an opportunity to make your own life as a software engineer easier. There may come a day, or many days, when you realize that you need their assistance. Having a friend or two in the system administration department is always a good thing. In my opinion, it's actually a good thing for there to be some communication between system administrators and software engineers, because the software engineers are the "customers" in one sense of the administrators. And it's always good to understand what the needs of your customers are.

Microservices

If I had to name one technology that has been one of the top three most important innovations in the development of web applications, I would say "microservices". It's so important and has become so widespread that I don't think it's a fad. From a certain perspective, it isn't something totally new. Rather, it takes existing technologies and looks at them in a way that makes web application software much more robust, scalable and easier to develop and maintain. And as we know, if a piece of software is easier to develop and maintain, that means that it will cost less initially and over the long run.

When I was first trying to read about the microservices approach, I struggled to get a clear idea of what it was and what it was not. There seem to be a number of slightly different definitions of microservices in the online literature. After having developed large software systems for many years using the "monolithic" approach, which I will explain in a moment, it can be hard to understand the concept of microservices at first. There is an abundance of material online that purports to explain what microservices are, and how they differ from other, older, approaches to web development. But I found many of them to be unclear and confusing.

Lessons Learned

Disruptive technologies don't necessarily have to involve the creation of something completely new. Taking a collection of existing technologies and coming up with a new approach that combines them in a better way can be just as powerful, if not more so, than developing a new technology such as a new algorithm or new language. If you are a software engineer, you should always be on the lookout for a new way to put existing technologies together in a way that improves some aspect of software development. Who knows? Perhaps you will be the inventor of a radical new approach that the industry will adopt for the betterment of all people who use computer technology.

Mobile Application Development

An area of software development that has grown steadily during the last couple of decades is mobile application development. Almost every major company that provide some kind of product or service now has a mobile app in addition to a website. It makes sense given the ubiquitous nature of mobile devices, especially smartphones. A perplexing aspect of mobile apps is that as they became more sophisticated in their features and technology, they also became harder to monetize. The norm nowadays is for mobile apps to be free. Very few apps cost anything to download and run.

Many of the technical challenges that used to exist when developing mobile applications have disappeared for become much less significant. For example, it used to be extremely difficult if not impossible to broadcast a message from a server to one or more cell phones. Today, this is a relatively easy thing to do. Most of the challenges that remain with mobile apps seem to relate to the limited screen area that an app can use to display information to the user. I suppose that will always be the case, until someone invents a way to show more information in a limited area.

Another challenge that has existed for many years with developing mobile apps is that you need to use specialized languages for programming them.

Lessons Learned

Mobile app development is one of those specialized areas of software development that are very important but hard to break into if you have no experience with them.

Obstacles

One of my favorite things that I used to hear from fellow software engineers or from members of management was "That's impossible, you can't do that! It'll never work." Whenever I heard those words, or something like that, I considered it a challenge to find a way to do whatever they thought was impossible. A common characteristic of most computer software is that it is almost always possible to find a way around any obstacle or limitation in some existing piece of software. Just because a software application, or language, or system, doesn't have some feature that would be nice to have, doesn't mean that you are stuck with the limitations of those technologies.

The great thing about computer software is that you can almost always build new functionality from old functionality, or write code that will modify existing functionality in some useful way. The question on one of my final exams that I had at Columbia where I had to define several software operations in terms of a single simple operation is a great example of this idea. If you are creative enough, there's almost nothing that you can't do with software. The main limitations usually are time, effort and cost. And you need to have the confidence that you will be able to find a solution. Without the confidence, you won't be able to be persistent enough to eventually find, or create, a solution.

For example, let's say that you wanted to write a stored procedure in a database, but you didn't want anyone to be able to read your source code. In some database systems, it isn't possible to "hide" your source code for stored procedures directly. However, if you create a stored procedure, and that stored procedure calls another stored procedure that does the actual work, then you can prevent people from seeing the code in that other procedure. So, if someone tries to view the source code for the procedure that you have made available to them, all that they would see is the call to your other stored procedure which has the source code protected from view.

Another way to get around certain limitations of web applications is to use a tool called a "monkey script tool". It lets you modify the HTML and Javascript code that is in a web page so that the page will do what you want it to do. This is very helpful when you are trying to add functionality to an existing web application, but you are not able to update the application itself. People who develop websites and web applications need to be aware of this kind of tool so that other people can't easily manipulate their web pages using tools like the monkey script tools.

Lessons Learned

There is almost always a way to get around any limitation or obstacle when it comes to computer software. The only thing that you need to do is keep looking for the solution, and you will find it eventually.

Office Politics

Pretty much any job at any company will have its share of office politics poking its nose into the work that needs to be done. The questions that we need to consider are "How does office politics affect software engineers?" and "How can software engineers become more aware of office politics and insulate themselves from its negative effects?"

One of the ways that office politics affects software engineers is by making it difficult sometimes to get the resources that you need to get your work done. I remember a project where I was responsible for composing some reports by writing code in a certain way, and the deadline was so close that I figured that I needed some help from someone else on the team to meet the deadline. As it turned out, one of the members of our team had some spare time on their hands, and I requested from my manager that they help me with the coding. Unfortunately, at the same time, another member of my team also needed help to get their coding work done on time, and they also requested the help of the same person that I had requested. This is where the office politics came into play. The other person on my team had more seniority than me, and was able to convince our manager that their work was a higher priority than mine to get done on time. The net result was a conflict over the limited resources of our team, and guess who didn't get their coding done on time.

Looking back on the events that transpired, I would say that possibly this situation could have been avoided if I had done a better job of estimating how long it would take to create the reports, and told my manager up front that the deadline date was unrealistic and not committed to it in the first place. The problem was that I had not coded those kind of reports before, and therefore I didn't have the ability to accurately estimate the time needed to complete them. This story illustrates how important accurate estimation is on a software project.

Lessons Learned

There is no way to totally avoid office politics. Rather than ignore it, try to learn as much as you can about how to prevent office politics from causing you pain as you work on your software projects.

Open Office Seating

One of the developments in office space configuration in recent years has been the creation of something called *open space*. This means that there are no separators between desks or seats, and everyone can see everyone else all the time.

The move to open space was gradual. First, cubicle walls started getting shorter. Eventually the walls in cubicles got so low that they were barely higher than the top of a computer monitor sitting on someone's desk surface. Then the walls almost disappeared. Finally, there were no more cubicles and just long tables with chairs on both sides for software engineers to sit in facing each other.

When I did coding work, I preferred an environment that let me concentrate on what I was doing and didn't make me have to deal with all of the distractions of an office environment where people are moving around and talking. Eventually, I did what many of my fellow software engineers did which was to wear headphones or ear buds to block out sounds. I also started listening to music to help me focus. I found that bluegrass banjo music tends to be equally loud throughout each song, and I listened to a lot of bluegrass. Unfortunately, headphones and earbuds are not able to block out visual distractions.

Lessons Learned

Figure out what works for you in each environment that you find yourself working in, but it's always good to have a nice set of earbuds handy to block out annoying noises and conversations while you are trying to focus on writing and testing your code.

Open Source

One of the major developments in the software industry over the last few decades has been the growth of open source software. This is software that is written by one or more people who are willing to make their source code public. Usually, the source code is available for free, subject to the users agreeing to one of many licensing agreements.

One of the benefits of open source is that you can see exactly what the code is doing because you have the source code and you can make enhancements and bug fixes yourself without waiting for someone else to do it. One of the problems with open source is the lack of technical support in many cases.

I remember being on several projects where open source software was used, sometimes as a small part of the project and other times as the central piece of the application. The main reason that companies used open source was to save money. In my opinion, using open source code in order to save money is a false savings in many instances. It's nice to think that you can look at the code and make fixes and enhancements any time you want. But who has the time for that? Being able to contact a technical support person with questions or to report bugs can save a lot of time and effort.

Lessons Learned

Be cautious about relying on open source tools and applications too much. Unless there is a very strong online community of volunteers to maintain the code and answer questions, it could end up costing you much more than you might expect.

Other People's Expectations

If you are the type of person who tends to factor in what others will think about you when making career decisions, my suggestion is that you refrain from doing that. For example, I thought that my parents would be very proud of me if I got promoted into management. Because of that idea, I expended a fair amount of effort over the years trying to achieve that outcome. Instead of figuring out whether a career in management meant sense for me, independent of what my parents thought, I kept devising strategies that I thought would increase the chances of me getting promoted into a management position in order to make my parents proud of me.

Eventually, I realized that my parents really didn't care exactly how my career developed and progressed. They were happy that I was employed and earning an honest living, and that was enough for them. It really doesn't matter what others think regarding one's career, including one's own parents. What matters is whether or not one's career progresses in a way that makes sense for that person.

Lessons Learned

Don't set career goals primarily in order to satisfy other people, including one's own parents. Make sure that your goals make sense for you. If people truly care about you, they will support you even if your career goals don't match what they think is best for you. It's your life, and your career.

Parallel Processing

Parallel processing or parallel programming is a computer software technique that can speed up the execution of computer programs, but it also has applications in daily living. This isn't really anything that new, but it is such an important concept that I fell it is worth mentioning.

The following are some examples of the application of parallel processing to real life situations:

• When preparing a meal, you can chop and cook the vegetables while the pasta is cooking.

• If you have to proofread a book with ten chapters, you could ask ten different people to each proofread a different chapter simultaneously, and then report the results when they are done.

As with most things, even parallel processing has its limitations. For example, if you have multiple CPUs or CPU cores in your laptop, you will be able to run multiple processes at the same time. However, you will still be limited by the number of CPUs or CPU cores. If you have four cores in your laptop, theoretically you could run four processes simultaneously and approach a fourfold increase in productivity. Similarly, if you have eight cores in your laptop you could do something similar and approach an eightfold increase in productivity. It's clear that if you have the resources available to process parts of your problem in parallel, then you should use them if you can.

The problem is that problems exist in computer science where the number of calculations that you need to do is so large that dividing that number by four, eight, or even sixteen won't provide the number of needed calculations to an order of magnitude that will allow your program to finish running within your lifetime. For those types of calculations, you need to do something else, like quantum computing, or perhaps something that hasn't been invented yet, that propels your ability to speed up processing many more times than just utilizing multiple CPU cores.

Lessons Learned

It's always good to know what the limitations are when running programs that are designed to calculate certain results, so that you don't undertake solving certain problems that will take so long that it just isn't worth doing.

Part-Time Work

One thing that I found during my last couple of years of full-time employment as a software engineer was that it is very hard to find any company that is willing to hire people part-time to do software development work. This situation was very puzzling to me. The number of open positions in high tech jobs seems to be rather high, and there aren't enough skilled workers available to fill those all of those job openings.

As a solution, why wouldn't companies consider hiring software engineers part-time? The work could be split up so that each part-time person would do about half as much as a full-time person, and two part-time people could be assigned to work on a task during a sprint that one full-time person could do.

Companies have become a lot more flexible regarding working remotely since the Covid-19 pandemic, although that trend appears to be reversing. Why not be flexible in the area of part-time versus full-time employment of software engineers? This would especially be helpful to older workers who have a lot of valuable experience, and at the same time are looking to improve their work-life balance. It seems like a winning idea to me, but for some reason companies have not warmed up to the idea.

Lessons Learned

If you are planning to work part-time as a software engineer, make other plans. There just doesn't seem to be a desire on the part of most companies to hire part-time technical talent.

Programming Language Idioms

I was given an assignment once to write a short program in Visual Basic. It was needed by another team that didn't quite have the resources to develop the program themselves, so I was tasked with writing it.

The problem that I ran into related to the style of the code that I wrote. I hadn't written any programs of any significant size in Visual Basic, and I went ahead and wrote some code that I thought fulfilled the requirements that were given to me. After I submitted my code to the other team, I received some rather negative feedback from them saying that the code was not very good.

When I asked them why they weren't happy with the code that I had written, the answer focused mainly on the style of the code, not the functionality. They basically said (pun intended) that it looked like I hadn't written much Visual Basic before and that it really showed. Well, I never claimed that I was an expert at Visual Basic, and I was happy to try to help that team out in their time of need. Even so, my efforts were not appreciated because of the way that the code was written.

Lessons Learned

Every computer programming language has its own "style", and if you want your code to be accepted among the coding community that uses that language, you need to learn generally accepted coding style as quickly as possible, and apply it when you do your coding. Otherwise, you will be seen as someone who is not a good coder in that language, even if you have lots of experience in other languages.

Quantum Computing

Quantum Computing is not something that I have direct experience with. However, I think it's worth mentioning because of its potential for making major changes in the way that computing is done, and because it is emblematic of what happens every now and then in the area of computer hardware.

There have been a number of significant developments in computer hardware over the years. I would say that there have been many more advances in computer software than computer hardware, but every now and then someone invents a new way of creating computer hardware that has a major impact.

One example is the GPU, a highly specialized computer graphics processor, that was originally developed for the video gaming industry to do certain types of calculations that need to be done very quickly and in large numbers. Someone realized that those specialized devices could be used to do the calculations that are needed for neural networks, now known as deep learning.

Quantum computing seems to be another one of those major development in computer hardware. Should software engineers start preparing to develop software for the new quantum computing hardware? I remember when supercomputers were developed and produced commercially. They ran so fast that it was difficult for companies to keep them busy running programs, which meant that it was hard to financially justify purchasing them. Since the current quantum computers are optimized for running only certain specialized kinds of algorithms, I think that it remains to be seen how widespread the impact will be in the field of software.

Lessons Learned

There appear to be many potential problems with quantum computers. If I were starting out on a career as a software engineer I would be very cautious about betting my future on quantum computing. But I would keep a close eye on developments in this area.

Real Life Software Development

There are many courses and books that teach various topics in computer science, and part of that instruction includes examples of code that accomplishes some particular task. Sometimes, a complete application is presented as an example. The problem is that the projects that you encounter in "real life", meaning those that you work on at a company or organization, are normally much more complex and involved than the small examples that are illustrated in the courses and books.

Of course, it is extremely difficult to include a complete, and realistic, software application example in the confines of a single course or book. So, the examples that you typically find are focused on the specific concepts or skills that the author is trying to convey. It would be great if there were some source of instruction that explained how an entire web application works, for example, as well as how to build such an application from scratch.

There are a number of differences between a real life software application and one that is described in a course or book. To begin with, there are the personalities of your coworkers that you need to deal with on a real project. There is also usually some "old code" that isn't working very well and needs to be either fixed or upgraded. In addition, real projects involve lots of meetings, communicating with management on a regular basis, various forms of testing, requirements that change every now and then, and so on.

Resume Writing

I have written and re-written my resume dozens of times over the course of my career. It would be interesting to make a video showing how it changed over the years, like one of those stop motion videos. I have also read and heard many ideas and opinions about how to write a resume, what information should be in it, how to format it, and so on.

These days, most resumes are probably filtered using specialized software that scans resumes and eliminates many of them before any human being ever gets a chance to look at them. I suggest that you read up on how the resume scanners work, and adjust your resume accordingly so that it can at least make it past the automatic filtering process.

Assuming that your resume will be read by a person, one thing to keep in mind is that the people who read your resume will assume that the item at the top of any list is the most important. Instead of just making a list of all of your skills, make sure that your best skills are at the top of the list. For example, if you are an expert in Java programming and the employer is looking for top notch Java developers, then there should be an item like "Expert Level Java Developer" at the top of the list of skills. But you need to be honest—if you have some Java programming experience, but you aren't an expert, then don't claim to be one.

Other useful advice that I've heard over the years include the following:

- Include numbers to highlight your experience. For example, instead of just saying that you have written a lot of Java code, it's better to say something like "Developed more than 25 complex Java applications."

- Always try to tell the reader what the net results and benefits of your actions were, not just what you did. For example, instead of just saying that you implemented an online e-commerce system, also say something like "The e-commerce system resulted in sales of over $1,000,000 in the first year of use."

- Always customize your resume to match the requirements of the job description as closely as possible. But you need to be careful with this approach because if a company sees more than one version of your resume and the versions are too different, they might doubt whether any of them are accurate.

- Above all else, be honest. Don't include work on your resume that someone else on your team did and try to claim it as your own. And try to avoid just saying that you were a member of a team that accomplished something—instead say what you did specifically as a member of the team and what you accomplished.

Lessons Learned

Writing resumes is a skill of its own and can take years to master. In today's job market, automated scanning and filtering of resumes is widespread. You need to write your resume in such a way that it can not only get through the filtering software, but impress a human reviewer as well.

Retirement—Don't Think About It!

I remember one job I was on where one of my colleagues used to keep a calendar on their desk. The calendar showed one day at a time, and each day they would set it to show the current date. At the top of each day's page in the calendar, that person had written the number of days until retirement. In other words, they were counting down the days until they didn't need to work anymore, and they could quit their job.

Looking back on it, I came to the conclusion that counting down the days to your retirement is a terrible way to approach each working day. You should certainly plan for your retirement as well as you can. But to keep reminding yourself every day that you are getting closer to being able to quit your job is not a great way to think about working. Instead, you should be focused on doing the best job that you can do, and continue learning new skills until the day that you actually retire. Then you can celebrate your career, relax, and enjoy not having to track down bugs in your programs anymore.

Lessons Learned

When I was in my fifties I decided to try running 5K races as a way to get into better physical shape. I wasn't that great at running, but one thing that I learned from those experiences was that you shouldn't think about slowing down or how much farther you need to run in order to get to the finish line. You need to stay focused on the here and now, on every step, and on every breath. It's the same with computer programming. Don't think about how many more years you need to work until you collapse from exhaustion. Focus on the present, but plan for the future.

Root Cause Analysis

When debugging a software defect and trying to locate where in the source code the error occurred, there is a concept called *finding the root cause*. I've noticed over the years that some companies emphasize this approach more strongly than others. But it is a great way to treat any issues that come up while a software system is operating in production.

The reason it's important to find the root cause or causes of a problem is that the error might be due to a logic error in the code, but it might also be due to some other problem that exists outside of the code and that has nothing to do with the code itself. For example, if you are developing a data ingestion system-that's a system that imports lots of data from various external sources-errors might be due to the external sources sending the data in an incorrect format.

What you want to avoid when trying to solve issues with software applications is to just make a change to the code so that the problem appears to stop. Doing so would amount to fixing the symptoms of the problem rather than discovering what's really causing the application to misbehave.

Lessons Learned

Determining what is really causing a software application to not function correctly can be very difficult and can consume a lot of time and resources. Having systems in place that let you monitor in detail the data that is flowing between your application and various data sources can help to solve many issues that are not caused by logic errors in source code.

Saving Ideas for Slow Periods

If you work in an environment where the amount of work to do is not constant, there is one thing that you can do to help yourself and the company you work for. This is especially handy when you are working for a consulting company that has a long-term relationship with a particular client. As you do your work, try to see whether there are any opportunities to develop a software application that would help the company or client. If you see such an opportunity, and it isn't something that urgently needs to be done, keep it in your "back pocket" and save it for later.

I did this once, the client liked the idea, and my company was able to do a small project for that client. The end result was that we maintained our relationship with the client, and went on to do other larger projects for them. By keeping us engaged, even though it was a relatively small project, we were able to continue providing needed software applications to them.

Lessons Learned

You never know when a "slow period" can happen, and there isn't much work to do. That's when you can pull out your idea for a software application and suggest it to your manager or client.

Exercise

Come up with an idea for a new software application or an enhancement to the application you are working on. Estimate how long it will take to develop and keep the idea handy.

Self-Confidence

Something that is essential to working as a software engineer is self-confidence. There are many situations where it isn't clear right away how to solve a particular problem, and if you don't have a sufficient amount of self-confidence, you will have trouble following through to find a solution. One thing that I learned over many years of experience developing software is that there is a solution waiting to be found for virtually any problem or requirement that comes up. It just might not be clear right away what the solution is.

The question is: How do you get the self-confidence that you need? I always struggled with this question, until one day I heard that when you do things, whatever it is, you gain self-confidence in that activity. In other words, a large part of self-confidence comes from the actual doing of something, rather than the thinking about it. If you try to instill self-confidence in yourself by just thinking to yourself that you have confidence, or by repeating the phrase "I am confident that I can do ..." in your mind over and over again, that by itself probably won't give you the self-confidence that you desire.

So, if just thinking about being confident isn't enough, how do you go about making yourself more confident that you can some any particular thing? I believe that the answer is that you just need to start doing that thing, and as you do it you will gain self-confidence. For example, let's say that you don't think that you can learn a new computer programming language quickly. What you can do it to pick any one of the dozens of languages that exist, and try writing a very simple program using that language. As soon as you start reading about the language, you will start

135

gaining some confidence. Once you have written a very simple program, you will gain more confidence. Time yourself, and see how long it actually takes you to do those two things. You might be surprised at how quickly you are actually able to do those tasks, and then you will realize that your fears about not being able to learn a new programming language were unjustified.

There are so many sources of information about computer software development available nowadays that there really is no excuse for not trying out new languages or any other new technology. If you are really having a hard time, you can always ask someone you know to help you get started learning about something new. But you will gain more self-confidence more quickly if you try doing it yourself.

Lessons Learned

Self-confidence is gained primarily by forcing yourself to do things that you don't feel confident or comfortable doing. By actually doing them, you will gradually gain self-confidence in those tasks. If you continue to take this approach throughout your career, then you will increase your chances of being more successful in your career.

Exercise

Think of something that you don't feel confident doing. Find a safe way to try it, where the consequences of failing won't matter. The act of doing that thing will help give you confidence to do it when it really matters.

Skills That Should Be Taught in School

If you are contemplating a career in software, or have recently graduated from a computer science degree program at a college or university, there are probably some skills that you have not learned in your classes but which are important to know. Here is my list of topics that tend to be overlooked in university degree programs for computer science, in alphabetical order:

Configuration as Code – This is one of those technologies that is very important when creating real world systems and applications, especially those in cloud environments. When you are writing small programs, you can get away without worrying about defining configuration files. But once you start working on real projects you will find yourself using this skill a lot.

Documentation – There are many ways to document all of the different aspects of the software systems and applications that you will be developing. Knowing how to use the various tools that exist for creating and maintaining the appropriate documentation will help you tremendously in your career.

Estimating – When you work on real software projects for real companies, real money is involved. The accuracy of your estimates will be a crucial factor in determining whether your project will be successful or not.

Interpersonal Communications – You must learn how to communicate both technical and non-technical information verbally and in writing. If you are nervous about standing up in front of a crowd and giving a talk, or even if you feel uncomfortable talking on the phone or on a video call about what you are working on, sign up for a communication class or join a group that helps people get over their fear of public speaking.

Learning a New Codebase – Any software engineer starting to work on a new project needs to get up to speed as quickly as possible on the entire set of code that makes up the project. The extent to which any particular part of the codebase needs to be understood depends on the role of the software engineer—for example, front end coders need to become familiar mainly with the front end code, and back end coders need to do the same with the back end code—but the speed at which the code becomes understood can have a huge impact on the success or failure of software projects.

Testing – There are many types of software testing. Pick up a good book on software testing and study it carefully. Software engineers are expected to do a lot of testing of their own code, and you can't rely on members of the Quality Assurance (QA) team to test your code for you. If you keep delivering code with defects to the QA team, you'll probably need to dust off your resume and start looking for another job.

Touch Typing – this is an essential skill for anyone who does a lot of typing regardless of what it is that they are typing. If you haven't already learned to touch type by the time you graduate high school, make sure to invest the time and effort to learn how to do it on your own.

Writing Large Programs – Software systems and applications in the real world tend to be very large and complex. They are usually too large to be developed by a single person. As soon as you can, either while you are still in school or after graduating from your degree program, try to get onto a project that is developing or maintaining a large piece of software. Corporate internships are one way to get some useful experience on large applications that is difficult to get at school.

Lessons Learned

If you are studying to be a software engineer or you recently graduated from a computer science degree program, it's important to be aware of all of the things that aren't taught in school. It's not a question of which technologies are being taught because there is a limited amount of time to learn and you can't learn everything in a short amount of time. It's more about the other kinds of skills that you need to learn in addition to the pure technical programming skills.

Small Versus Large Software

When you create a piece of software, you need to decide how many and how much of the known software engineering principles you should apply when developing the code. If the number of lines of the program is very small, then perhaps it isn't necessary to create all of the infrastructure, use standard coding styles, apply the DRY principle, and so on. For example, if the program is small enough that there isn't any need for the same logic to be applied in multiple places in the code, then the DRY principle doesn't really apply since there isn't any logic to repeat. Certainly, if you are creating a large software application, then as many of the software engineering principles that you can apply should be applied, in order to make the code more readable, maintainable, testable, documentable, and on and on.

The interesting question is, "Is there a certain size of a software application where it transitions from being a tiny program, which doesn't need lots of software engineering principles applied to it, into a large program which definitely will benefit from all of those principles?" And if there is a point of transition, what is it and how do you know when you have crossed that dividing line?

From what I've experienced, that imaginary line of separation between small and large software applications has gradually moved closer to the small size. In other words, in today's software development world, even a very small program should be developed using the same set of tools and techniques that are used to develop larger applications. In fact, many of today's software applications are built by creating many small pieces of code where each small program does an essential function, for example in the development of a microservices application.

Lessons Learned

In today's software development environments, it is best to always apply all of the latest software engineering principles and techniques regardless of the size of the program. This will help ensure that every piece of code is tested thoroughly, documented well, stored properly in a source code repository, and ready to be deployed as needed by means of an automated deployment process.

Sprinting to the Finish

One of the modern techniques used by teams of software engineers is something called a "sprint". A sprint is usually a mini two-week project that results in either a small enhancement in functionality or a collection of bug fixes to an existing software application that is already running in a production environment, or to a new software application that is under development and has not yet been released into production. The time frame could be as short as one week and could be as long as a month.

The idea of working in sprints is part of the approach to software development called "Agile". Before this approach became popular, software development teams could work for months or years on a new version of a software application before releasing it into a production environment. Doing so made it very difficult to manage, and many times would result in lengthy delays and cost overruns. One of the reasons for that is due to something called *scope creep*. What tends to happen on many projects, especially web applications, is that users keep thinking of new features they would like the application to have. And if they are really good features, the developers can have a hard time saying no to the users because they are afraid that the users won't be satisfied with the application otherwise.

A downside to working in sprints is that not everyone is comfortable with working at the same pace. Personally, I like to not feel pressured to deliver a whole feature or set of bug fixes within a very short time frame. I would rather work on a larger piece of functionality for, let's say, two or three weeks, then spend a few days testing it and then submitting it to the QA team.

You need to understand that if the sprint lasts for two weeks, that doesn't mean that the software engineers have two weeks to develop and test their changes. Most likely they will only have at most a week to do so, after which they will need to deliver their coding changes to the quality assurance team on the project so that they can fully test the changes before moving them to an integration or production environment. And, if the QA team finds any problems with the code during the second half of a two-week sprint, then the software engineers will only have a day or two to fully resolve any problems and resubmit the code to the testing team for re-testing before the end of the sprint.

Lessons Learned

Agile software development and short sprints appear to be the favorite way to develop software these days. It's just a fact of life for software engineers. Unfortunately not everyone works at the same speed and the agile approach to coordinating teams doesn't seem to accommodate differences in coding speed among team members. One way to handle this challenge is to try to keep the scope of each sprint small enough that even slow coders will be able to complete their tasks within the time given.

Software Recipes

A software recipe is a step-by-step description of how to get something done using software. I have found it very helpful to create two kinds of software recipes, or *how to* lists.

The first kind of recipe shows how to accomplish something using a particular software tool, perhaps using your programming editor or debugger. Many times you will need to execute a complicated sequence of keystrokes and commands. Instead of trying to memorize the sequence, it's best to document the list of steps needed. The second kind of recipe describes the steps involved with doing some complex procedure, such as all of the steps needed to deploy a code module to production. Again, instead of trying to memorize the sequence, write it down.

Lessons Learned

There are two main benefits of documenting the steps you need to take in order to accomplish a useful task:

- If you don't need to do the sequence often, but it is important to know how to do it, documenting the recipe saves you the time of researching how to do the thing each time you need to do it instead of memorizing it.

- Documenting sequenes of steps allows you to share them with the rest of your team, so that they don't need to waste time figuring out how to accomplish the task each time.

Exercise

Think of a recent complex task that was difficult to memorize, document the steps involved, and share them with your team.

Starting Over

Let's say you start working in the computer software field, and it's going well at first. You are excited to be working with the latest software technology and you are really enjoying the work. After a while, perhaps a few years, or perhaps several years, you might begin wondering about making some sort of major change in your career. The problem with making too big a change in your career, especially if you are already several years into it, is that there are already many people with a lot of experience in those other areas that you might want to compete with. And they probably have advanced degrees. For example, data scientists are frequently required to have a PhD and a large number of published articles.

A major change could be one of a few different types. You could be looking to

• change the focus of your technical software development work from one area of expertise to another area of expertise;

• move into the area of system administration of cloud computing environments;

• change you role from a software engineer to a user experience specialist who designs the user interfaces of web applications for web browsers and mobile devices;

• get into the data science field; or

• leave computer software technology completely and pursue some other very different field like law, medicine or finance.

The above potential major changes are listed in order of increasing difficulty, in my opinion. I don't consider learning a new programming language to be a major change, so it's not included.

Moving from one area of software expertise to another area, such as going from doing the backend development for web applications to doing front end coding for the same kinds of applications is probably the easiest way to make a significant change. It will give you the opportunity to try out different areas of software technology that you have been aware of, but were just not able to spend time working on.

One advantage that software engineers have within the data science realm is that they have learned what is generally called "software engineering techniques" for creating efficient code, version control, managing deployments, and so on. Many people in the data science area have backgrounds in statistics, and know how to apply various modeling techniques for making certain types of predictions, and similar types of applications of statistics to data. However, not all data scientists have the same kind of experience in "software engineering" techniques that software engineers have.

Trying to leave the field of computer technology completely, and pursue a totally different line of work can be extremely difficult, and potentially disastrous for your career. If you really have your mind set on making this kind of change, at least try to do it early in your career. In many cases you will find that you will need to completely start over from scratch, and build your career back up to the level that it was before you decided to make a change.

For one thing, you will likely need to take a very large pay cut since you will have almost no experience in that other field. And you might need to go back to school and earn another degree, possibly a master's or PhD degree. If you have other people in your life who depend on for their financial support, then this alone could be the reason that will make it totally impractical to completely change careers. It's much better if you can at least figure out which general area of work you want to get into for the long term when you are in high school or college. It just makes things so much easier.

Lessons Learned

Once you've spent a significant number of years in the software field, you might start thinking about switching careers. If you try to switch into certain other fields, such as working in the financial investment world, you are likely to get the response, "Sure, you can start at the bottom and work your way up". The problem with this is that starting at the bottom usually means taking a very large pay cut.

This was the experience that I had. The further along I was in my software development career, the more difficult it became to start over from the beginning in some other career. If you are not happy doing the work that you are currently doing as a software engineer, perhaps you need to change your focus and keep working as a software engineer rather than jumping out of software development entirely. The smaller the change, the easier it will be to adapt and thrive in your new role. Gradually making small changes rather than one giant change will give you time to learn about your new focus and grow into it.

Working as a software engineer requires a major commitment

of time and energy on your part. If you are not prepared to be in the field for the long term, then you might be better off working in a different area.

Exercise

Make a list of the reasons why you got into the field of software development in the first place. Do all of those reasons still make sense? Which ones don't seem to be relevant and more? Next, make a list of other areas of software work that you are interested in and which will build on the experience you've gained so far in your career. Finally, create a series of small steps that you can take to get you from where you are now to where you want to be.

Startups

Startups can sound like exciting places to work, but they also have their downsides. One of those downsides is the instability of the job, especially if the initial funding of the company is running low, and the company isn't generating much revenue.

One startup that I worked for was created based on an idea for an innovative software product. It was technologically advanced, and I enjoyed working on it. What I didn't realize when I joined the company was that it had already burned through a large percentage of its funding. Eventually, the company laid off most of its employees and I needed to find another job. Looking back on the experience, I should have done a better job of finding out how far along the company was on its startup journey before accepting a position there.

Another experience I had was an in-person interview with a startup that seemed to be relatively stable. After a long interview, the hiring manager sensed that I might not be happy working in a very fluid environment and told me that the leader was prone to making sudden changes in direction for the company. Such changes could cause any project that I would be working on to end suddenly or undergo drastic changes. I agreed with the manager and thanked him for his comments. Looking back on that situation, I think it would have been too unstable an environment for me and I was happy that the manager was open and candid about the working conditions within the company.

Lessons Learned

Working at a startup is not for everyone. Startups have a lot of potential for success, but also have a lot of risk. Great ideas are just ideas until they are implemented and proven in the marketplace. If you want to have a stable job and steady career progression, think twice before joining a startup. And make sure to ask how much funding they have received, how much of that funding still exists, how many customers they have for their products or services, and how much revenue the company is generating. If the management at the company either can't or doesn't want to answer those questions, beware.

Conditions can change suddenly and without warning at a startup—even if it is well funded—depending on the person leading the company. If you do decide to work for a startup, make sure you have a plan B in case the company folds or has a massive layoff. And be ready for sudden, drastic changes on any of your assigned projects.

Statistics and its Importance

Anyone who develops software these days should be familiar with statistics, both the theory as well as their application to real life situations. When I was in college, I took an introductory course on statistics, and I remember thinking how boring the subject was. The textbook was boring, and the lectures didn't really get me excited about wanting to learn statistics and how to apply them. I had a vague idea that statistics was an important subject, which is why I enrolled in the course in the first place, but it wasn't until many years later that I realized how important they really are.

Data science is built on statistics. If you are thinking of getting into the area of data science, you should definitely become familiar with as many statistical techniques as possible. But even if you are not planning to become a data scientist, knowing statistics can help you become a better data analyst. Being able to analyze the data in your application's database can be very helpful.

Lessons Learned

Even if you find the idea of statistics boring or unimportant, make the effort to learn at least the basics of statistics. There could be many opportunities to apply your knowledge of statistics to the data used by the software applications that you develop.

Stress Relief

One of the projects I worked on was very stressful, to the point where we were really feeling it. Our small team had to keep learning new tools and technologies at a very rapid pace during the project. At some point one of our team members suggested that we play a soothing song whenever the stress got to be too much. We settled on the song "Don't Worry, Be Happy" by Bobby McFerrin. It worked. Any time we felt the stress hovering over us, one of us would play the song and it would make us all relax.

Lessons Learned

If you, or your team, are feeling extremely stressed while working on a project, consider playing some relaxing music to reduce everyone's stress level.

Exercise

Find a variety of songs that make you feel relaxed. When you are feeling stressed on a project try playing one of them and see whether it helps. Make sure to use headphones or earbuds so you don't bother anyone else. If your team seems to be stressed out, suggest playing one of your relaxing songs for them and see whether everyone's stress level goes down.

Technical Terms Keep Changing

One common theme that I noticed in my software journey is that many of the technical terms used in the industry have changed over the years. Sometimes the change implied an actual change in meaning or the underlying technology. But many times a term has changed primarily for political reasons, and not because of any significant technological innovation.

Programmer, Developer, Engineer

For example, the term for the job of computer programmer has changed from *computer programmer* to *software developer* to *software engineer*. At one point in the early 2000s, the term *programmer* was used to mean someone who could write computer programs to meet a given specification, to distinguish it from the term *developer* which meant someone who could not only code but also design the application. There were even separate Java certifications for Java Programmer and Java Developer. But I think that the distinction has grown less important over the years, because nowadays software engineers are expected to write programs to meet given specifications, and at the same time to make sure that the code being written fits into the overall design of the system being developed. In addition, today's software engineers are expected to thoroughly test their code, with the goal being that no defects should be detected by the quality assurance specialists.

When I went on interviews for the role of senior software engineer, companies would want to hear about any software design experience that I might have had. And they would place a lot of emphasis on that aspect of my work experience. The problem is that in many corporate environments, not everyone on the

153

team has the opportunity to do much design work. Many times, a software architect has already established the fundamental design of the software application under development, and there isn't much additional design work that is needed. Rather, lots of code needs to be written to implement lots of functionality and many unit and integration tests need to be written to ensure software quality. And all of that code and the accompanying tests need to fit into the design that the architect has already created.

Lessons Learned

I think the software industry has settled for now on *Software Engineer* as the standard way of referring to someone who develops software. But don't be surprised if some new term comes along soon to replace it.

Database, Data Warehouse, Data Mart, Data Lake

Many terms have developed to refer to various kinds of databases. A whole book could be written about this topic. The rate at which new kinds of databases are being created has accelerated within the last ten years or so. For many years, the relational database was the main kind of database available. They still have their place in the world of software applications, however many specialized ways of storing data have been developed since then.

Lessons Learned

Data storage and retrieval has always been an integral part of any software system or application. But in today's environment, many specialized kinds of databases have been created. It is important to learn about all of them at least to the extent that you know what features they have and which kind of data storage system is the most appropriate for the application that you are developing.

Exercise

First, make a list of all of the kinds of data storage systems that you are familiar with or are aware of. Then search the web for as many kinds of data storage systems that you can find that are not on your list, and make a separate list of them. Finally, commit to learning enough about each of those systems so that you can intelligently choose which one would make most sense in any given situation that you might face as a software engineer.

Deep Learning

If you've been trying to keep up with the latest developments in Artificial Intelligence (AI), you have probably come across the term *Deep Learning*. This is a very good example of a technical term that was created recently, but which actually refers to a technology that has been around for a very long time.

There used to be a term called Neural Networks, which referred to a method of imitating the way that the neurons in the human brain seems to work. I remember reading about it and buying books on the subject thirty years ago. The problem with neural networks was that the number of calculations needed to produce any significant results was so large that computer technology couldn't process them fast enough.

Now that computer technology has advanced to the point where those calculations can be performed within a reasonable amount of time, the use of neural networks has grown immensely. However, now the technology is called Deep Learning. Why the change? I attended an AI conference a few years ago, and one of

155

the speakers explained that the old neural networks had gotten a bad reputation because of the lack of raw computing power. A new term needed to be create in order to help give the neural network idea a fresh start, and the new term is deep learning.

Accelerator

A word that I've heard a lot in the last decade and which I think has become overused it *accelerator*. When you first hear the word it certainly sounds great. Who wouldn't want to accelerate the pace at which they are innovating or developing? The problem is that if a word is overused, it loses its power. In the tradition of one of the old methods of creating acronyms, we could create one called YAA, meaning Yet Another Accelerator.

Lessons Learned

Be cautious when people use the term *accelerator*. The word sounds terrific, but it's been overused and now could mean almost anything.

That's Why They Call It Work

There will be times in your career as a software engineer when you will work on very interesting projects which will keep you mentally engaged in tackling new challenges and learning new technical skills. There will also be times when you will need to work on something that provides no challenges and doesn't force you to grow in any way. It's actually a good thing to have a mix of interesting and not-so-interesting projects, because sometimes you need time to let your *learning self* take a rest.

There may also be times when the uninteresting work drags on for a long time, and it starts getting annoying. You feel like you want to learn something new, take on some kind of challenge, or just do something a little different. Those are the times when you need to tell yourself "That's why they call it work", meaning that you just need to do whatever it is that you are getting paid to do, and don't complain.

Lessons Learned

Working as a software career has its ups and downs. You can't expect every project and every assignment to be exciting, challenging, and inspirational. Sometimes you just need to get the assignment done—making sure that you do it well—and then move on to the next one.

Theory Versus Practice

Sometimes knowing the theory behind some computer technology is helpful, and other times it isn't that helpful at all. It's important to be able to recognize when the theoretical foundations of any particular technology are worth studying, and when they aren't.

One example of theory that is useful is what's known as the CAP theorem. It basically tells you that no matter how hard you try when designing a distributed system, which is a collection of servers that store data and can execute programs that process that data, it is impossible to achieve high levels of consistency, availability and partition tolerance. The point is that if you are given the task of designing a distributed system and you are not aware of the CAP theorem, then you might try to build a system that has high levels of all three things, and create a system that is seen as a failure. If you are aware of the CAP theorem, then you will first decide which two of the three things you want to achieve, and then design and build your distributed system accordingly.

An example of theory that isn't very helpful to the practicing software engineer is relational database theory. I once bought a book that went into excruciating detail regarding the theory that underlies relational database systems. In order to read and understand that book, you had to be comfortable reading and understanding mathematical theorems and proofs. But in order to use a relational database system, you only need to understand the practical aspects of the database and how to achieve the results that are needed. Relational database systems are built on a foundation of relational database theory, but knowing the theory is not a prerequisite for being able to use a relational database.

Things My Managers Taught Me

I've had many managers in my career, and to be honest many of them were rather annoying and didn't help me be the best employee I could be. But, over the years I discovered that many of my managers taught me something useful that I kept in mind for the rest of my career. This section contains some of those things my managers taught me.

Software Project Trade-offs

One of my managers taught me that any project has three main aspects that you need to manage: Cost, Time, and Quality. In general it is extremely difficult to complete a software project for a low total cost, in a short amount of time, and with very high quality. At best, you can expect to achieve two of the three aspects. For example, if you keep the cost too low, then you will be limited in the quality of the software engineers that you can put on the project and the quality of the software will be low. Or, if you can try to get the project done too quickly, then quality will suffer because of all of the mistakes and errors that will creep into the code due to the rushed nature of the requirements gathering, computer programming and software testing work. Finally, if you insist on a level of quality that is extremely high, then it will tend to lengthen the time needed to fully test and approve the software before putting it into a production environment.

This idea, that there are three aspects to something, and that it is very difficult to achieve high levels of all three at the same time, is reminiscent of the theory in the area of distributed transaction processing systems called CAP Theory. The initials CAP stand for Consistency, Availability and Partition Tolerance.

159

According to CAP Theory, you can achieve only two of those three aspects of a distributed transaction processing system, where a distributed transaction processing system is defined as a collection of servers that are networked together and operate as a single transaction processing system.

In addition, I remember hearing this rule about job hunting: There are three major factors that relate to trying to decide whether or not to take any particular job: The Work, The Pay, and The Commuting. The theory is that it is extremely difficult, though not impossible, to find a job that has high ratings in all three areas. The rule is that if you can find a job that has at least two out of the three factors in your favor, then you should seriously consider taking the job. It's up to you to decide whether you are willing to take a job where the work itself is not that interesting or valuable for your career development, where the pay is less than ideal, or where the commuting is very long and tiring.

Perhaps there is a "two out of three" reality underpinning much of computer software development, and not all of those types of rules have been discovered yet. It's probably good to keep an eye out for those sorts of things, and maybe you will formulate a new "Two out of three" rule yourself one day and become rich and famous, or at least famous.

Decision Making

When you are trying to make a decision, regardless of what the decision involves, always try to figure out all of the possible options. Then, you can pick the best one among all of the available options. You still need to make a good judgment regarding which option is the best, but at least you reduce the chances of finding out later that there was a much better option available that you didn't even consider.

Prioritizing Tasks

I had a manager who introduced me to the concept of the Four Quadrants of Covey. The basic idea is that you can plot all tasks that you need to accomplish on a graph which has two axes. One axis is the Importance of the task, and the other axis is the Urgency. Then, you split the graph into four quadrants such that every task falls into any one of the following:

- Urgent and Important

- Urgent and Not Important

- Not Urgent and Important

- Not Urgent and Not Important

Once you categorize everything that you need to do into these 4 quadrants, you can see clearly which tasks you should be spending your time on, and which tasks you should avoid, or put off until later.

Clearly, the tasks that are urgent and important should be done right away, and have the highest priority. Also, it's clear that tasks that are not urgent and not important can be delayed indefinitely without causing much harm, and these should be your lowest priority tasks.

The other two remaining quadrants are the interesting ones. If something is not important, but is urgent, like responding to a phone message from a salesperson so that they won't keep bothering you, then it's fairly obvious that you should only handle those tasks when you have some spare time.

The tasks that are not urgent, but are important, are the ones that people tend to ignore, since they aren't that urgent, but will cause problems in the long run if they are ignored. For example, learning new technical skills. This leads us to the next great idea, which is continuous learning.

Treat Your Coworkers as Your Customers

There can be a temptation sometimes to ignore communications from your coworkers due to shortness of time or other normal stresses in the day to day work of a project. But it is important to treat everyone that you work with as your "customer" in order to make sure that the project moves forward smoothly. And you should consider it your job, among other things, to make sure that your coworker "customers" are happy and content with whatever they need, assuming that you are able to provide the things that they are requesting.

Keep Learning and Growing

In the long run, it is critically important for anyone doing software development, who wants to avoid becoming obsolete, to regularly devote some time to learning new skills, and improving existing skills. It is only by spending time regularly over a long period of time that you can stay up to date on your technical skills. Don't expect to get caught up on all of the innovations that occur constantly around us by just spending one or two days, or even a week, per year on training.

Another manager introduced me to online learning websites, which have a very large supply of courses on almost any technical subject that you might be interested in learning. Several years ago, many of the courses offered by these online educational websites were free of charge, and if you wanted to pay an optional fee you could receive a certificate of completion to show your boss or put on your resume. Now, in 2024, most of those websites charge at least something for their courses, either an annual fee or a separate fee for each course. The good news is that there are many such websites, and you can shop around for the best deal. Many times they will have special sales, and you can sign up for courses at a very low cost. It pays to keep an eye on all of those websites and have specific courses in mind that you want to enroll in. When the price is reduced, jump on the opportunity! Before signing up for an expensive, all-inclusive membership, it's probably a good idea to try out just one of the courses first, and then if you discover that the website has many great courses that you know you will want to take, then it might be worth paying for an annual "unlimited course" subscription if there is one available.

I remember, when I had my summer programming job at IBM while I was in college, one of the managers advised me to keep learning and growing, especially in areas that you might not have thought of originally. I didn't think much of it at the time, perhaps because the pace of technological change in the 1970's was not as fast as it is now in the 2020s, and it didn't seem as "urgent" a thing to do. But I can still hear him in my head telling me that good advice. It was good advice then, and even better advice now.

Don't Copy and Paste Code

One of the lead software engineers on one of my projects gave me some great advice which I tried to follow as well as I could for the rest of my career.

One of the common rules in computer programming is

known as DRY, which stands for Don't Repeat Yourself. It basically means that you should avoid having the same logic repeated in multiple places in your programs. If you realize that the same logic needs to be executed in various places, then you should create a "reusable" piece of code that can be invoked as needed, wherever it's needed.

When it comes to writing code, which is basically "executable text" written in a programming language, it is very tempting to just copy a few lines of code and paste it into another place in your program. One of the problems with copying and pasting these little snippets of code is that the program becomes harder to maintain. If you realize at some point that there is an error in the logic, or you decide that you want to modify the code to make it better or run faster, you have to find all of the places where you have pasted the snippets, and update all of them.

But Do Copy and Paste Other Things

A project manager of mine once pointed out that there are times when it is good to use the copy and paste feature on your computer. One of those times is when you need to use some expression or word that is difficult to spell correctly. Instead of typing the word every time you need to use it, and risking making a typo that could have large negative consequences, just copy and paste it. I've seen many computer programs where the name of a data variable that stores some useful value appears in different places with slightly different spellings. What probably happened was that the programmer didn't copy and paste the variable name, and instead they kept typing it and making small typing errors every now and then. This kind of error can be very difficult to detect, and it can cause some very strange behavior in your software.

Don't Be Afraid to Speak Up

One of my managers towards the end of my software engineering career pointed out to me that it seemed to him that I was reluctant to speak up in certain situations and express my opinion about certain things. He wasn't sure why I was doing that, but perhaps it was because I had built up a fear of something bad happening if I said the wrong thing.

The problem is that in many situations it can be very difficult to predict how people will react to what you plan to say, and if you experience a lot of negative reactions to whatever you are suggesting then you might naturally be reluctant to keep doing that. In my case, apparently I had gradually become less and less daring in making suggestions or expressing my opinion on various aspects of the projects that I was working on.

Lessons Learned

It's important to express your opinion about the things that you are working on, even though there is a risk that you might say something that others won't like and your position on a project could be jeopardized. You need to be thoughtful before speaking up, but at the same time you shouldn't be so cautious that you end up saying almost nothing.

Trends

One of the most important things that software engineers need to do as they progress through their careers is to be aware of all of the trends that exist and how they might affect the field of software development. When the Java programming language first came out in the mid-1990's I had a feeling that it would start a major long-term trend, and I was right. I rode the Java wave until the end of my career with much success.

Lessons Learned

Trends are your friends. You need to keep in touch with your friends and not ignore them. Trends in software technology come and go, and can either be short-lived or long-term. But they are almost always relevant to your career.

Even though software engineers are usually focused on technology, don't forget about business and economic trends. They can have as much impact or more on your career than technology trends. For example if the industry that you are working in is experiencing a major long-term economic decline, you should be looking at other industries that are more robust.

Exercise

Maintain a list of trends that you are aware of and update it regularly, at least once every few months, as you detect changes in existing trends and the creation of new trends. Group trends into categories such as: Technology, Economy, Industry, Employment, Salary.

Two-Out-of-Three Method

How can you decide whether or not to take a job offer? A related question is, how can you compare one job offer to another? Someone told me the following rule, and I've used it many times to evaluate job offers.

The rule is based on the idea that every job has three main aspects to it: the pay, the commute, and the work itself. In other words, the pay can be very good or not so good, the commute can be short or long, and the work can be interesting and challenging, or boring and dull. The rule says that if a job opportunity has at least two out of those three aspects, then it is worth taking.

The above rule is based on the assumption that it is very hard to find a job opportunity that excels in all three aspects. Instead of waiting for the perfect job where the work is fascinating, the pay is amazing, and the commute is very easy, one should be willing to take two out of three. In my opinion, the most important aspect of all three is the work itself. So, I would modify the rule slightly and say that if the work sounds good, and either the pay is good or the commute is good, then it's worth taking the job.

Updating Software

Almost any software that you use, whether it is the operating system on your laptop, the accounting software that you use to do your bookkeeping, the version of Java that is installed on your computer, or virtually any other software application or utility, will eventually need to be updated to the latest version. Some software applications and utilities need to be updated very frequently, while others require updates only rarely. Regardless of the frequency of updates, all kinds of software will need to be updated at some point.

The question that arises is, "Should I apply the updates?" To many people, this might seem like an unusual question, because if an update is needed, why not go ahead and apply the update? And probably most people routinely update their computer operating systems and any installed software applications. After all, the manufacturer of the software is telling you that you need to make the update, so why wouldn't you?

The answer is that installing updates to operating system software or other software that applications depend on can suddenly stop working after the update in applied. For example, there are many software applications written in the Java programming language. In order for Java applications to run, an underlying Java runtime package needs to be installed. Recently, Oracle decided to release new versions of the Java runtime package four times a year. This is a much faster rate of change in Java versions that before. How can a software development team keep up with all of the new versions of Java and make sure that all of their code will continue to run correctly?

An example of dealing with this challenge in an automated way is the Amazon AWS tool called Amazon Q Code Transformation which aims to automate the process of making necessary coding changes to Java applications whenever a new release of Java occurs. I expect that other similar tools will be developed by other companies in order to help software development teams keep up with the dizzying number of applications that need to be checked and upgraded every time a new version of some underlying software is released.

Lessons Learned

All software applications run in some sort of environment and typically depend on one or more underlying software runtime packages. It is critically important to be aware of whatever dependencies your software has on other software and be prepared to spend the time and money to upgrade your applications whenever needed. Things that can alleviate some of the work include reducing the number of underlying software runtime packages that are used on a project and using tools that help to automate the process of upgrading application software.

Vacation Time

Vacation time (called *on holiday* time in Europe), is an important part of the overall computer programming experience and is especially important if you are an observant Jew. Having always observed the prohibition against working on the major Jewish holidays, I found myself in a continual struggle to get enough paid days off to celebrate the Jewish holidays and have some other days off for just relaxing. You see, if you observe all the Jewish holidays that prohibit work, there can be years in which a total of thirteen vacation days are needed to satisfy the requirement of not working on the Jewish holidays that occur on weekdays. So, if you are only getting two weeks' vacation, or ten days, that isn't enough to cover the Jewish holidays without even considering any other days for relaxing or stress reduction. I've found that most people in the corporate world who are not Jewish don't realize that if you observe the Jewish holidays which prohibit working on those days, then you are not really "relaxing" on those days off. Those days off have many restrictions which don't allow you to enjoy the typical vacation activities that anyone else could enjoy.

Recently, the concept of *unlimited vacation* or *unlimited PTO* has been gaining popularity at many high-tech companies. Supposedly the idea is that as an employee you are entitled to an unlimited number of paid days off, to be used as you see fit. I never actually worked at any of those companies that offered unlimited vacation, but my understanding is that it is a great idea for the companies and not such a great idea for the employees. Even though it sounds like you could take off as many days as you want, it will ultimately be up to your immediate manager to decide whether or not to approve your actual number of days off.

Another aspect of vacation or PTO time is that even if you are guaranteed a lot of paid time off, say twenty days per year, you might not be able to use those days when you want to due to the requirements of the specific project you happen to be working on. One unpleasant situation happened to me where I was hoping to attend a significant family event, but I was told by my manager that I could not take the time off because a production release of a new version of the application I was working on was scheduled for the weekend immediately after the days that I wanted to take off. And because of the timing of the production release, he would not allow me to go on the family trip. As it turned out, the production release went smoothly with no problems, without requiring my involvement at all. I could have gone on my trip without it causing any issues. But when your manager has the final say on when you can take time off and is not willing to be flexible, there really isn't much you can do about it. One of the benefits of working for yourself, which I am enjoying now as an independent writer and book publisher, is that you have much more freedom to decide when you get to take time off and spend quality time with your family.

One more thing that I want to mention regarding vacation time is that the best, and perhaps only, time that you can negotiate more vacation time for yourself is when you are considering an offer for a job. Once you are on the job, it is much more difficult to get more vacation time than the official number of days offered by the company. I learned this the hard way. There was a job that I had found through a headhunter, and it didn't have quite as many vacation days as I had hoped for. The headhunter advised me to take the offer, and then plan ask for some additional days off several months later after doing a great job. Unfortunately, that never happened. I took the advice of the headhunter and

171

accepted the job. When I eventually asked for a few more days off, I was told that the company had a very strict policy for vacation days and there was no way that they could increase them just because I wanted them to.

Lessons Learned

The best time, and perhaps only time, to ask for the number of vacation days that you really want is when you are negotiating the terms of an offer. You need to know how many days you must have to be happy. If a company is not willing to give you the time off that you want, you can try offering to take a slightly lower salary in exchange for some more vacation days. But if that doesn't work, you need to be willing to walk away from the opportunity. Otherwise, you will be putting yourself into a situation where you will be unhappy as long as you are working for that company.

Sometimes, the advice that headhunters give is not necessarily in your best interest. You need to remember that the headhunter makes their living by placing you in a job, and the headhunter is primarily looking out for themselves, not for you. Once you are in the job, you are on your own and you won't be able to fall back on anything that the headhunter said to you about the job. It is your responsibility to make sure that you find out as much as you can about the job and not to rely on any statements from headhunters.

Unlimited vacation time can sound enticing, but don't be fooled into thinking that it is truly unlimited. Realistically, you won't be able to actually take off more than a normal number of days, however "normal" is defined within the industry, since the work of the job needs to get done.

Version Control

Keeping track of all of the versions of your code has always been a challenge. However, the way that people dealt with this challenge has changed quite a bit over the years.

The simplest way of keeping track of versions of your code as you develop a software application or system is to just create separate folders or directories to keep each set of files, and to label the folders with appropriate names. This is how I remember first handling multiple versions of code that I had developed. If you are dealing with a small piece of software and you create very few versions, this method can work. But it's a very primitive way of doing so, and will ultimately lead to various problems and difficulties.

One of the important tasks that you need to perform when working with multiple version of your code is to be able to go back to earlier versions and see what changes were made between one version and the next. This is important because it helps you to zero in on the possible locations for errors that can creep into your code as you create new versions. If you make a couple of small changes somewhere in a very large set of files of source code, and then you realize that something is not functioning correctly either because an automated test failed or by some other means, you need to be able to quickly locate the changes and see whether any of them caused the unexpected, incorrect, behavior in your program.

In the early days of coding, people developed special programs that could compare text files and tell you where the differences were. These became known as "diff" programs or tools, and over time they became increasingly sophisticated in detecting and showing the changes that occurred. Eventually, these tools were incorporated into the modern source code control systems that make it easy to keep track of all of the versions of your code.

Various other improvements were made over time, such as storing the code on each programmer's computer and allowing the programmer to "push" their changes to a central repository system that stored the "official" version of the body of code. Systems that store publicly accessible repositories of source code have become very popular as the amount of "open source" code has grown very large. Nowadays, being comfortable using the most popular source code control systems has become a fundamental skill required of all software engineers. If you are just getting started in your programming career, make sure you know how to use all of the features of the latest source code control systems very well. It is an investment in time and effort that is well worth it.

Visual Programming

At various times in my career, I have come across programming tools that were created to make it easier for non-programmers to write code. The approaches of these tools consisted mainly of representing various programming concepts in visual form, based on an assumption that seeing little pictures with lines connecting them is easier for non-technical people to understand compared to lines of code. In my opinion, some of those tools were more useful than others, and even the best of them were of limited helpfulness.

The tools in this category that are the least useful, in my opinion, are the ones that simply replace the keywords in a programming language with pictorial icons that represent the keywords. Instead of writing code using the actual keywords, you create a collection of these little pictures and draw lines or arrows between them to indicate the flow of the program. The problem with this approach to visual programming is that the person using the tool still needs to think like a programmer and figure out the sequence of steps that the program requires to take in order to calculate the desired result. In fact, if you are able to write a program using one of those visual programming tools, you could just as easily write the code just using a normal programming language. Your program would take up a lot less space on the screen, and you wouldn't need a special tool to write a piece of code.

When Nothing Seems to Work

Every now and then, no matter what I did to fix a problem, it just refused to be fixed. Being at my wit's end, I would call over a colleague to take a look at the code that wasn't working. On many occasions, while I was showing the ill-behaving code to the other software engineer, the code would suddenly start working correctly. It appeared as though someone else just looking at the code would make it work correctly. I can't explain this phenomenon, but if you ever are in a situation where things just aren't working no matter what you try, call over another person to take a look. There is a small chance that doing so will somehow cause the problem to go away. Perhaps the act of showing your code to someone else causes you to do something subconsciously that fixes the problem.

Lessons Learned

There is almost always a rational way to fix any issue that occurs with software. But sometimes it takes an unusual act, like having someone else take a look at the code, in order to make it work.

Why Does the Opening Exist?

When you are looking for a new position, and you hear about a specific opportunity at a certain company, it's always good to find out, if you can, why the opening exists. There could be many reasons why a particular position is available, and depending on the reason, you might or might not want to pursue it. Determining the true reason, or reasons, can be very difficult, but it's worth the effort to try.

For example, it could be that there is an opening because the person who was doing the work was so frustrated with how things were going on the project, or within the company in general, that they quit and went to work somewhere else. If that's the case, you need to tread cautiously because you could be the next person leaving that company after you discover what is really going on. Again, it's usually very hard to determine whether or not this is the case, and even if it is, the person who left might have left for all sorts of reasons which won't have anything to do with whether or not you will fit in and enjoy working in that position.

If you determine that the opening exists due to strong growth within the company or within a particular project, then that is usually a good indicator that the position doesn't have any negative baggage associated with it. You will still need to figure out whether the opportunity is a good fit for you, but at least you will know that the job was created due to a positive change within the company.

It's also good to know whether there are multiple openings within a department or team, and that job that you are interviewing for is one of those multiple openings. If there are multiple openings, that increases the chances that you will be able to join the team. When a company is looking to add several people to a project, they usually are looking for people with a variety of skill sets and experience. Multiple openings also usually indicates that the company has enough money in their budget to hire more than one person, and it's always a positive thing if the company that you are looking to work for has money to spend on projects.

Working From Home

There has been a raging controversy recently in the year 2024 whether working from home is a good thing or a bad thing. I've seen strong opinions expressed on both sides of the issue, although the trend seems to be that the number of companies asking their employees to come back to the office either most or all of the time has been increasing. The whole issue arose because of the Covid-19 pandemic, which caused a lot of businesses to close their offices and ask their employees to work from home.

Is working from home a good idea for software engineers? My answer, like many things in life, is "It depends". Each person has their own ideal work environment. Some prefer to work closely alongside others in an office setting, while others prefer to work in a secluded area where there are no distractions so they can concentrate. I tended to fall into the second group, so whenever the opportunity arose to work from home I took it.

Is working from home a good thing for companies who employ software engineers? Over the last year or two I've seen an increasing number of news articles about high tech employees who figured out how to be employed by multiple companies without any of them finding out. Working from home, or the beach, makes it easier to avoid detection. When a company requires employees to work at the office five days a week, it is easier for them to monitor their employees. Unfortunately, a growing number of people have been taking advantage of their remote work situation and they are spoiling it for everyone else.

In my opinion there are a number of advantages to allowing employees to work from home. Those employees are not necessarily isolated from their fellow team members. There are many more ways for people to be in touch today than there were decades ago. And many projects span multiple time zones and multiple countries. There just isn't a practical way for all of those people to sit together in a physical room and do their work even if they wanted to.

Collaboration is more about communicating and helping each other succeed than it is about being in the same room or office. In my opinion, software engineers can do amazing work regardless of where they are located, whether it's in an office or at home. As long as proper security can be provided and the work gets done, the physical location shouldn't matter.

Lessons Learned

It's hard to go against a major trend, and one of the major trends that I see happening now is the gradual movement of employees back to the office. There are good arguments that can be made on both sides of the issue, and each company and each employee will have to work out what will happen.

Conclusion

Having experienced the growth of computer technology during the last four decades like a surfer riding waves of innovation, I hope that you will find the experiences and lessons learned in this book helpful to you as you proceed on your own career journey as a software engineer.

Perhaps you will be writing a book like this twenty, thirty, or forty years from now, providing software professionals the benefit of your experience and wisdom. Who knows whether software engineers will even exist forty years from now. The rate of change in computer technology has been so rapid recently that it's become almost a full time job just to keep up with the changes.

I think that whatever you do, try to be flexible and ready to adapt to changes in the technology itself, and to changes in how industry and individual consumers use computer technology.

And if the stress of rapidly changing technology ever seems like it's too much to handle, take a short break. Brew yourself a fresh pot of coffee. Listen to some calming music and relax. But don't relax for too long. You might miss noticing a new software technology that was just invented which will dramatically change the world.

Career Summary

In this section I provide a summary of my career in software develoment. I spend a disproportionate amount of space on my college experience and my first job, but that's because they provided the foundation for everything that followed.

My career began when I majored in Computing Science at Columbia College in New York City in the late 1970's. Back then it was called Computing Science and the major was offered by the Mathematical Statistics department. It was only after I graduated with my bachelor's degree that Columbia College created a Computer Science department along with a brand new Computer Science building and offered a Computer Science major.

During my junior and senior years in college an amazing transformation took place in the computer hardware and software that was used and taught at Columbia University. When I first started writing computer programs in the second half of my sophomore year, everyone use punched cards to write their programs which were run on IBM mainframe computers. There were special machines that created a card with holes punched in it for each line of code in a computer program. Then those stacks of punched cards had to be fed into a special card reader that frequently jammed. Every now and then someone would drop a stack of cards on the floor and would have to put them all back in order before feeding the stack into the card reader again.

All of that changed dramatically in my junior year. Minicomputers were introduced to the campus, and all of the punched card machines disappeared. Interactive terminals appeared and with them a new operating system called UNIX.

Even the programming languages changes markedly within a two year period. When I began coding we were using the FORTRAN programming language. Then there was BASIC. There was also the PL/I language that tried to blend the scientific nature of FORTRAN and the business nature of the COBOL programming language. By my senior year we were using C language. It all happened so fast. At least it seemed as though computer technology was changing rapidly. Looking back on it now, it's obvious that the rate of change in the area of computer technology continued to increase during the last forty years and will probably continue to increase at an even more rapid pace in the coming years.

One of the things that I learned in college that had practical application to real life was the searching algorithm called Binary Search. It only works on data that is already in sorted order, like the names in a phone book. You have to remember that in Manhattan, where Columbia College is located, in the 1970's the printed white pages and the yellow pages telephone directories were extremely large and thick books. Because they were so large, it could take a long time to locate a person's name or a business name. Using binary search, you could find it very quickly. Today, you just do an online search and can find the same information almost instantly.

My most difficult Computing Science course at Columbia College, and perhaps the most difficult course I took for my entire bachelor's degree, was Graph Theory. A graph is a set of nodes, or points, which are connected by lines called edges. I had heard about graph theory before, and I knew a little bit about it. In elementary school I remember our math teacher talking about the famous seven bridges problem which is a graph theory puzzle. But I wasn't prepared for the grueling proofs that we had to understand and develop on our own in that college course.

There are many theorems in graph theory that sound very simple, and it's not that hard to understand what they mean. But when you are given an assignment to prove a theorem in graph theory, it can be extremely difficult. Especially if you aren't used to doing proofs. Sometimes it's just very hard to figure out how to approach proving any particular theorem, and then to follow through the proof from start to finish.

Some professors are able to teach even during a final exam. I remember getting a very interesting problem on a final exam in one of my computing science courses. The problem involved using a simple computing operation, that was defined in the body of the question, to create other more useful and more complex operations. In other words, you had to think creatively on the spot to devise new computing operations from simpler ones. We had not discussed this idea in class, so it forced us to think on our feet under the time pressure of a final exam. And it showed that a lot of computer logic can be built up from smaller, simpler pieces of logic.

That exam problem showed that one doesn't need to create all of the logic from scratch to solve a problem, and that one can take smaller pieces of logic and put them together in interesting ways to define larger, more powerful logical ideas. This exam problem gets to the essence of the power of computers. At their most basic level, computers operate in a world of ones and zeros, and simple logical operations like *and, or,* and *not.* On top of those basic operations one can build tremendously complex thought patterns and computer systems.

185

After graduating from college I landed a job as a computer programmer at AT&T Bell Labs in New Jersey. But I only worked there for a few weeks over the summer, and then went on to study at the University of Michigan in Ann Arbor for my master's degree as part of the special program at Bell Labs known as the OYOC (One Year On Campus) program.

My ten months at the University of Michigan in Ann Arbor studying for my master's degree exposed me to a side of computer technology that I had not seen while an undergraduate at Columbia University. Pursuing a master's degree in the interdisciplinary subject of CICE (Computer, Information, and Control Engineering) allowed me to fill in more of the computer hardware knowledge that I didn't learn in the courses I took for my bachelor's degree.

Bell Labs had a great reputation and I was happy to have landed a job there. So much so that I didn't really care which part of the company I worked in or exactly what I was doing. I assumed that the work itself would be very interesting and challenging, and would provide me with useful experience for the future of my career.

After working at Bell Labs for a year or so I met someone who had started working there around the same time I did, and who was working in one of the advanced software departments. During one of my conversations with him he revealed to me that when he was in college he had learned about that department and focused his job searching efforts on becoming a member of that specific department. That's when I realized that I could have done a better job of looking for a job. I was just happy to be working at Bell Labs, but he had a specific interest in the work being done within a specific part of the company.

186

When I joined Bell Labs, I was assigned to a software development team. As I recall, it was somewhat of a disappointment for me since the work involved writing code to move data from one place to another. It would take data that was typed on a screen and store it in a database. In fact, most of my career ended up writing code to move data from one place to another.

At some point, I realized that there was a team of people doing testing, meaning that they were checking the software for any incorrect functionality. I was intrigued by this idea, and looked into it. When I suggested to my manager that I might be interested in joining the testing team, he was quite happy and welcomed me into his team. Only later did I realize that the vast majority of software developers, then and probably also now, would rather develop software than spend time devising testing strategies and doing large-scale software testing. It seemed to me that there was a certain bias against software testing as a profession, as though it was a lower form of intellectual activity, and not challenging enough.

I found testing to be a fascinating area of work, and I delved deeply into it. Even in the early 1980's the level of sophistication of software testing was quite high. People were using terms like black box testing, white box testing, functionality testing, performance testing, and load testing. We even had the concept of calculating the percentage of a program's source code that was executing by our tests, commonly known as coverage testing. The tools that are available today to help with software testing do very similar things to the tools that existed back then.

After a couple of years of software testing, however, I realized that if I kept doing it for too long, it would make it difficult for me to get other work in the future as a software developer. Most hiring managers who were leading software development teams were looking for people with lots of programming experience, and didn't care so much about one's testing experience.

I found the idea of writing code that just stored data in a database and allowed the user to retrieve the data at a later time to be a little boring. I discovered that our project had a testing team whose responsibility was to test the software and discover any hidden bugs in the code. This sounded interesting to me and the idea of testing software to find any hidden bugs triggered a positive reaction in me.

I explored the idea of moving from the coding team into the testing team and was welcomed openly by the manager and the team. I was very excited and decided to switch into the testing team. It was only later that I found out that the vast majority of software programmers did not want to do full-time testing, and in fact they looked down on anyone who wanted to do testing.

After I left AT&T Bell Labs, I worked at a few companies during the period of 1987 to 2004. I stayed at each company for only a few years. Looking back on my experiences during that time, I think I was changing companies every few years for a number of reasons.

First, I was trying to increase my salary. I determined that if I stayed too long at one company, my salary would not increase much. After you've been with a company for a certain amount of time, and the company feels that you are happy working there, they will tend to slow down your salary increases to save money, figuring that if you are happy working there you won't want to leave. The most reliable way of getting a significant salary increase seemed to be to change companies.

Second, I think I tended to get bored easily and the easiest way to work on something new and exciting was to change companies. At one point I challenged myself to stay at the same company for more than two or three years, and I stayed at one company for six years just to prove to myself that I could do that.

During those years, in the mid-1990's, the Java programming language was just beginning to be used. I was very excited about the Java language because it allowed a programmer to create object-oriented programs without having to deal with some of the problems that other object-oriented programming languages such as C++ had.

By the beginning of my later years as a software engineer, starting around the year 2002, after trying out a few different types of software development to satisfy my desire for variety I was ready to try to stabilize my career and not move around from company to company as much. I was just passing my mid-40's and I was noticing that many of the people I was working with were a lot younger than me. The trouble was that at the same time that I was looking for more stability in the software field, the rate of change in computer technology seemed to keep increasing, and it was getting harder and harder to keep up with all of the innovations that were being made in the industry.

While I was working at a startup in the insurance industry, I heard about the pharmaceutical industry, and the idea that many of the companies in the *pharma* industry, as it is commonly called, have very good cash flows and thus are able to employ a large number of people. People would say that if you can get a job at one of the pharma companies, it would be relatively stable compared to many other industries.

Even though I didn't have any background in pharmaceuticals, and from what I had heard it was very difficult to break into that industry, in 2002 I joined a medium sized company that provided specialized computer services to pharma companies. While I was there, I noticed that certain software systems were used very commonly within the pharma industry, and one in particular was the Oracle database system. I already had a good amount of experience developing software that used the Oracle database, so I think that my experience with that technology helped me to gain entry into the pharma industry.

I decided to keep working within the pharma industry and in 2004 I landed a job at a small consulting company that did custom software development for pharma companies, mainly in the areas of data warehousing and custom web application development. Even though I didn't have much experience with the main functions of pharma companies, and I had never worked within a pharma company, the consulting company was willing to take a chance on bringing me into their world. My first project was a small very successful one, and many more projects kept me employed there for almost ten years.

By the time I was getting close to fifty years old I started thinking that perhaps continuing to work primarily as a software engineer would not be the best thing for me to do as I got older. It was clear to me that an increasing percentage of my co-workers were a lot younger than me, and it was getting harder to keep up with all of the changes in computer software technology. So, I looked into the area of project management.

One the things that seemed attractive about project

management (PM) was that it didn't matter what kind of software you were working on, or which industry you were in, there was always a need for some kind of project management. There was an established body of knowledge relating to project management, including a large standards body and well-recognized certifications for PM. I even took a course on PM and studied to take the certification test.

Ultimately, after thinking about it for quite a while, I decided not to pursue a full-time PM role. I realized that if you enjoy working with software and creating new applications, then you won't feel comfortable without the hands-on experiences that a software engineer role provides. Project management is a very important function, and it is essential that projects have at least one person who is in that role. But, one of the things about project management that make it a little uncomfortable for many software engineers is that it requires a fairly high level of people skills. If the idea of being a manager doesn't thrill you because of all of the time you need to spend interacting with other people, then you might not be very happy as a project manager either.

In my mind, project management does not involve a lot of technical innovation. That's where the software engineers and software architects come into the picture. Developing software in the modern world requires almost constant innovation. On the other hand, PM is all about applying standard ways of tracking and managing projects in order to complete the project on time, within budget, and with the expected level of quality.

I worked for the last few companies of my career from 2014 to 2022. It was during these years that I pushed myself very hard to keep learning new things, and to keep up with the very rapid changes in software development.

A number of headhunters that I spoke with during that time period told me that they were very impressed with the fact that I was pushing myself to keep learning and growing, especially at my age. A number of developments in online learning helped me to keep up with advances in technology, and I took advantage of them as much as I could.

During the last few years of my full-time software career, I expanded my programming language expertise to include Python and Kotlin, both very important languages for today's software engineer. I also got involved with the whole area of cloud computing. I decided to focus on AWS (Amazon Web Services) initially. I earned a few AWS certifications, including some of the specialized ones, and I worked on projects that involved AWS technologies. Later, I also got some experience using the Microsoft Azure cloud system. Cloud computing is a vast area that has many potential subspecialties. If I were still working as a software engineer I would probably want to work in some area of cloud computing.

Index

Princeton 90
prioritize 41
programming puzzle 10, 11
Python 101, 102

resumes 31, 130, 131
retirement 132
root cause 133

scope creep 142
self-confidence 135, 136
society 9, 109, 110
startup 67, 84, 149, 150
statistics 146, 151

team lead 12
testing environments 52

ABOUT THE AUTHOR

James N. Gershfield received his bachelor's degree in Computing Science from Columbia College in 1979 and his master's degree in Computer Engineering from the University of Michigan in Ann Arbor in 1980.

After working at AT&T Bell Labs as a Member of the Technical Staff for eight years, he spent the next thirty-four years working as a software engineer at a variety of companies in several industries. His last project ended in 2022.

Since then he has been writing, editing, and publishing books.

www.ingramcontent.com/pod-product-compliance
Lightning Source LLC
Chambersburg PA
CBHW071213210326
41597CB00016B/1801